Columbia University

Contributions to Education

Teachers College Series

No. 223

AMS PRESS
NEW YORK

TESTS OF LITERARY VOCABULARY FOR TEACHERS OF ENGLISH

BY

LAURA HALL VERE KENNON

Teachers College, Columbia University
Contributions to Education, No. 223

Bureau of Publications
Teachers College, Columbia University
NEW YORK CITY
1926

Library of Congress Cataloging in Publication Data

Kennon, Laura Hall Vere, 1888-
  Tests of literary vocabulary for teachers of English.

  Reprint of the 1926 ed., issued in series: Teachers College, Columbia University. Contributions to education, no. 223.
  Originally presented as the author's thesis, Columbia.
  Bibliography: p.
  1. Vocabulary. 2. Mental tests. 3. English literature--Study and teaching. I. Title. II. Series: Columbia University. Teachers College. Contributions to education, no. 223.
PR35.K4 1972   153.9'4'4281   70-176966
ISBN 0-404-55223-4

Reprinted by Special Arrangement with Teachers College Press, New York, New York

From the edition of 1926, New York
First AMS edition published in 1972
Manufactured in the United States

AMS PRESS, INC.
NEW YORK, N. Y.   10003

ACKNOWLEDGMENT

It is most difficult for me properly to express my thanks to the members of my Committee and to others who by their advice, encouragement, and practical aid made this study as free from fault as it is. I am deeply indebted to all the members of my committee, and to Professor Allan Abbott, in particular, for continued encouragement and wise, friendly counsel. My thanks are due also to Professor Arthur I. Gates in appreciation of his criticism and suggestion, and to Professor Thomas H. Briggs, finally, for critically valuable analysis of certain difficulties along the way.

I am grateful to my friend Dr. Faye Huntington Klyver for generous help in long hours of scoring and to Dr. Ella Woodyard for her advice in statistical matters and her unstinted help. For his always sound advice, and for permission to use the Thorndike Intelligence Examination, Part III, I express my thanks to Professor Edward L. Thorndike.

L. H. V. K.

CONTENTS

CHAPTER	PAGE
INTRODUCTION	vii
I. THE IMPORTANCE OF VOCABULARY AND OF LITERARY BACKGROUND FOR TEACHERS OF ENGLISH	1
II. THE MAKING OF THE TESTS	14
III. THE RELATION OF LITERARY VOCABULARY TO OTHER ATTAINMENTS	26
IV. CONCLUSIONS	34
APPENDICES:	
A. The Experimental Forms of the Tests	37
B. The Specific Literary Sources of Test Words	43
C. Alphabetical Lists of Test Words with Order of Difficulty	57
D. Words in Order of Difficulty by Permilles as Used in Published Forms A and B	63
E. Complete Tables of Data	65
BIBLIOGRAPHY	77

INTRODUCTION

The whole subject of vocabulary and vocabulary testing has been considered, particularly in the case of school pupils, from almost every conceivable angle. There are certain things known about the relationship of children's vocabularies to their developing thought and intelligence; differences in vocabularies of individuals have been found and charted; the rate of quantitative growth, the relation of quality to extent of vocabulary, and the estimate of total vocabulary known for a given age or grade have been subjects of study and research.[1] Not so much has been done, however, in the higher levels of vocabulary, in the specialized word knowledge of fields like English and history, or with groups of adults who were working in some particular field of interest. It may be informing and helpful to know among other things just what kind and amount of word knowledge related rather specifically to the field of English literature is the possession of teachers of English; and further, to discover what relationships exist between word knowledge related rather specifically to the field of English literature, and other attainments of teachers of English as shown by their academic preparation, by their experience in terms of years, by the positions they hold, and by certain measures of intelligence and achievement.

It is the purpose of this study to present two forms of a literary vocabulary test for teachers of English which will serve as one means of exploring word knowledge related specifically to the field of English literature, and to show the relationships existing between actual word knowledge revealed in the results from these tests, and certain measures of intelligence and achievement.

---

[1] Terman, L. M., *The Intelligence of School Children*, pp. 308–312, and *The Measurement of Intelligence*.
Terman, Kohs, S. C. and others. "The Vocabulary Test as a Measure of Intelligence." *Journal of Educational Psychology*, Oct., 1918.
Thomson, G. H. *Instinct, Intelligence and Character*, Chap. XII.
Thorndike, E. L. *Vocabularies of School Pupils*. Contributions to Education, New York Society for the Experimental Study of Education, Vol. I, p. 74.

TESTS OF LITERARY VOCABULARY FOR TEACHERS OF ENGLISH

CHAPTER I

THE IMPORTANCE OF VOCABULARY AND OF LITERARY BACKGROUND FOR TEACHERS OF ENGLISH

To teachers, in general, and to teachers of reading and English, in particular, the task of helping in the development of pupils' rich and meaningful vocabularies has been appointed. From the kindergarten to the senior high school there are standards set and programs suggested to aid in developing and extending meaning vocabulary and accuracy in word recognition.[1] The prime importance of vocabulary in the whole field of English and language study is now conceded in any discussion of the subject. Dewey's chapter on "Language and the Training of Thought,"[2] widely known both in its original setting and as the basis for much of Inglis's discussion on "The Aims and Values of the Study of Language,"[3] is a classic reference which can again be cited, particularly when it is examined with reference to the special field of the teaching of English.

What Dewey has to say on the enlarging of vocabulary is important not only for the teacher in his relation to the pupil, but also in his own "intellectual enterprises" since "intellectual life depends on possession of a store of meanings."[4] His point is, that the successful modification of "speech habits into accurate and flexible intellectual instruments" can be accomplished by "(1) enlargement of the pupils' vocabulary; (2) rendering its terms more precise and accurate, and (3) formation of habits of consecutive discourse."[5] Inglis carries on this discussion under the development of habits of consecutive thinking and consecutive discourse, saying "The development of an extensive vocabulary in which the extrinsic meanings of terms are adequately mastered, is an extremely difficult task of great importance in

---
[1] *Twenty-fourth Year Book of the National Society for the Study of Education.* Part I. Report of the National Committee on Reading, Chap. IV.
[2] Dewey, John. *How We Think,* Chap. XIII.
[3] Inglis, Alexander. *Principles of Secondary Education,* Chap. XII.
[4] Dewey, John, *op. cit.,* p. 174.
[5] *Ibid.,* p. 180.

secondary education."[6] If one accepts Inglis's statements as expressing sound and desirable aims and values in the study of language, he would doubtless also subscribe to this statement: "Precision and accuracy in thinking and in the expression of thought is vitally conditioned by precision and accuracy in word uses. Increase in the precise and accurate use of words is no less important than the increase in the number of words more or less at one's command . . . However extensive his vocabulary may be, unless it is characterized by precision and accuracy and definiteness in use for thinking and expression, it must fail to be an efficient instrument for those processes, and must lead to looseness and error in thinking."[7] And having subscribed wholeheartedly for the pupil, why should not one even more carefully sign again for the teacher of English, one of whose tasks it is, to see to it that the development of vocabulary, both extensive and intensive, is accomplished?

Another admirable expression of opinion as to the importance of word knowledge for teachers of English, and one based evidently on the same underlying principles, is this paragraph from a letter by Walter Lippman, which serves as a preface to a report on "The Teaching of English in the Large Cities of the United States":

On the teachers of English our society depends for the formation of habits of speech, which are in reality habits of thought that will equip the modern citizen to give precision to experience by naming it. Our social life depends on the presence of enough people who can tell different things apart and discern identities where they exist. It depends, therefore, on people who use words without confusion as to their meaning, to whom the name of this and that is the name of this and that, and not of half a dozen vaguely related things as well. It depends on people, who in language at least are what the Mediaeval schoolmen called Nominalists, on people who do not mistake general terms for objective facts, on people who can penetrate phrases like Bolshevism, socialism, democracy, liberalism, radicalism, Americanism, and can arrive at candid, vivid understanding of the particular persons, acts, hopes, fears that these omnibus words are supposed to cover.[8]

Teachers of English ought, reasonably enough, to be able "to tell different things apart and discern identities" in the vocab-

[6] Inglis, *op. cit.*, p. 433.
[7] Inglis, *op. cit.*, p. 432.
[8] *The Teaching of English in Large Cities of the United States.* A Report, with an Introductory Letter by Walter Lippman. Published by the New York City Association of Teachers of English, Oct., 1922.

The Importance of Vocabulary & Literary Background

ulary of their chosen field of English literature. The name of "this and that" ought clearly to them to be the name of "this and that," particularly since many of them have spent some years ostensibly in learning the identities and differences involved in such discernment. An English teacher ignorant of special literary vocabulary is as much an anomaly as a school psychologist unaware of the laws of learning, a lawyer unacquainted with the law, or a farmer unacquainted with the cycle of weather and crops. In the words of Inglis, again, "there is a necessary parallelism between the development of vocabulary and the development of clearly defined percepts, concepts, feelings of meaning, and the like. The development of individual meanings cannot proceed very far without the development of the corresponding vocabulary." [9] If the teacher of English, then, is especially responsible for the enlarging and enriching of school pupils' vocabularies, he has not only the need of vocabulary for his own intellectual enterprises, but also the need of wealth of vocabulary to increase, rather than "to shut down the area of mental vision of his pupils." No teacher of English would wish to have quoted concerning him, "Paucity of vocabulary on the part of those with whom the child associates . . . tends to shut down the area of mental vision." [10]

The enlargement of vocabulary takes place "by wider intelligent contact with things and persons, and also vicariously, by gathering the meanings of words from the context in which they are heard or read." [11] Surely it is fair to say that teachers of English have, in general, the same, or, at least, ample opportunity for the acquisition, by either of these methods, of vocabulary in the specific field of English literature. Opinions of experts in the field of English teaching agree as to the desirability and value of literary training for teachers of English. Acquaintance with English literature, begun with its study in grade and secondary schools, is broadened and enriched through college, especially by those who make adequate and intentional preparation for the teaching of English by doing their major work in English and related fields. The teacher of English at work with his classes renews his acquaintance with literature which was in many instances a part of his own college entrance

[9] Inglis, *op. cit.*, p. 426.
[10] Dewey, *op. cit.*, p. 181.
[11] Dewey, *op. cit.*, p. 180.

4   Tests of Literary Vocabulary for Teachers of English

requirements in English. The worth and importance of this background of literary subject-matter is presented through the following quotations concerning the desirability of acquaintance with English literature as a requisite in the sound preparation of teachers of English.

In a chapter, "The Training of the Teacher," in *The Teaching of English* (Carpenter, Baker and Scott), Scott says:

. . . it is important that the teacher of English should be we'l read in English literature and English literary history. That he should have expert knowledge of the whole range of literature in English is of course out of the question; but he ought at least on the one hand to have made a careful survey of the entire field and to have acquired definite ideas of the course of literary development, and on the other hand to have formed an intimate acquaintance with the leading English classics. As regards the history of literature, the greatest danger is perhaps that the teacher will rest content with biography and history instead of pursuing the study of literature itself.

. . . Again, as regards literary masterpieces, the greatest danger is that the teacher will mistake vague recollections of the utterances of critics, more or less eminent, for acquaintance with the works themselves. What is needed in this particular of his training is, first, appreciative reading, which through sympathy will bring the reader into the closest possible contact with the mind of the writer, and then critical reading, which through the exercise of the judgment will reveal the technical sources of the writer's power.[12]   (1903)

Chubb repeatedly gives as the "chief burden of our counsel." that

. . . what we chiefly need for the improvement of our English teaching is a broader, richer, and more thorough literary training and culture for our teachers. It must be insisted that they shall be . . . generally well read in the great classics (absolutely necessary to the formation of taste and judgment), and in the history of, at least, English Literature.[13]   (1903)

Professor Baker in an article [14] discussing a suitable equipment for the teacher of English gives the following as the second section of an answer to this question, "What, under conditions not yet ideal, may we set up as a working standard?"

. . . A special training in English, both in literature and language. This means, of course, a full knowledge of the great things in our literature, a fair

---

[12] Carpenter, Baker, and Scott. *The Teaching of English*, p. 310.
[13] Chubb, Percival. *The Teaching of English*, pp. 360-61.
[14] Baker, Franklin T. "The Teacher of English." *The English Journal*, June, 1913.

The Importance of Vocabulary & Literary Background

knowledge of much of the second rate, and above all a scholar's sense of relative values. . . .

In his outline of a general course for the preparation of teachers of English, Gaw notes these which might well be included:

(a) an introductory course for training in intelligent reading, clear thinking, and effective writing, the basis being standard novels, dramas, essays, and verse;

(b) a course in the general history of English literature from Beowulf to the present time;

(c) a course in the general history of American literature;

(d) an intensive course in Shakespeare;

(e) intensive courses in one or more other periods of English literature chosen with due regard to the superior claims of the last two centuries from the high school point of view.

. . . To these might be added as advisable late electives in the English field courses in (j) the novel, (k) the drama, and (l) the history of criticism.[15]

In answer to the question "What subjects shall we choose?" Thomas among other things says:

. . . there are certain authors that should be carefully studied. The most important, of course, are Chaucer, Shakespeare, Milton, Pope, Wordsworth, Carlyle, Browning and Tennyson. And these should not be studied for their works merely; they should be studied in relationship to the times in which they lived, the movements they helped to further, and the general influence which they exerted upon their contemporaries and upon the future trend of literature. . . He (the student) should .. . . plan to take a thorough course in American literature. (1917) [16]

In the bulletin, "Reorganization of English in Secondary Schools," page 149, appears this suggestion for the literary elements of "reasonably standardized courses":

(1) studies in the nature and elements of the various literary types, in addition to a broad reading knowledge of English and American literature. (1917)

Under the caption of "much genuine experience of excellent literature," Leonard says:

Certainly acquaintance with all the poetry and drama and fiction which are great and simply understandable enough to be inc uded in good high-

---

[15] Gaw, Allison. "The Collegiate Training of the Teacher of High School English." *The English Journal*, May, 1916.
[16] Thomas, Charles Swain. *The Teaching of English in the Secondary School*, pp. 296-97.

school lists of required reading . . . and some comprehension of why these things have been accounted great, is surely a fair requirement for every teacher to make resolutely and earnestly of himself. It is highly to be desired, of course, that he really know, as well—by his own intelligent reading, and not by report and lecture only—the materials collected in survey courses in literature, particularly if he is in charge of junior high school classes in English.

It seems impossible to suppose that anyone will teach literature adequately in senior high school without a real familiarity with material read in the common period courses given to undergraduates, and very desirable is a thorough acquaintance, preferably in graduate study, with at least one period of English literature.[17] (1922)

In the answers to question 7 of the questionnaire sent out to high school teachers by Professor Baker's Committee on the Preparation of High-School Teachers of English (1915), a suggested "list of courses in English of special value to the prospective teacher of English" included these under the head of literature: Short Story, General Course on the Types of Literature, The Novel, The Essay, Poetry, The Drama, Periods of Literature, American Literature, World-Literature, Contemporary Literature, Shakespeare, and Criticism.

As one of the results of an investigation reported by H. G. Paul,[18] these paragraphs are one more indication of what is considered good college background:

Of the possible additions to the college curriculum, desirable for teachers of English, the chief demands are for five courses: (*a*) an advanced survey of English literature; (*b*) a course in primitive literature; (*c*) a course in comparative literature; (*d*) one in contemporary English and American literature. . .

As an irreducible minimum for the teacher of English, the consensus of opinion favors the requirement of the bachelor's degree from some reputable college. The necessity of at least courses in a survey of English literature, in Shakespeare and American literature . . . is emphasized.

To anyone who has been long concerned with the preparation of teachers of English these opinions are perfectly familiar; they are grouped here again only to call to mind the emphasis placed on the generals and the particulars of literary background considered at best a somewhat limited equipment for the novice, to be added to in all seasons by diligently reading on and on.

[17] Leonard, S. A. *Essential Principles of Teaching Reading and Literature*, p. 65.
[18] Paul, H. G. "The Preparation of High School Teachers of English." *The Bulletin of the Illinois Association of Teachers of English*, Feb., 15, 1915, p. 17.

Granted the desirability of a rich background of English literature as one element in a sound college preparation for the teaching of English, there is to be considered the accessibility of such riches. The extent and kind of courses in literature open to the prospective teacher of English, or an acknowledged part of the preparation of those already engaged in teaching, are quite as important as "the irreducible minimum of the bachelor's degree from some reputable college." In order to find some indication of present college offerings, and the provision made for special teachers' courses, a study was made of a chance selection of fifty college catalogues for 1923-1924.[19] Table I shows the kind and the extent of the offerings of those colleges listed under English literature, arranged to show both the frequency of occurrence generally and the number of specific courses offered by each college. Related courses, advised or required as electives, and courses in rhetoric, composition, versification, short-story writing and journalism were omitted. This table shows that American literature is offered by forty-five of the fifty colleges and that Shakespeare, Drama, English Novel, Chaucer, and a survey course are offered by over half the number. By far the largest numbers of courses are offered in the earlier periods of literature with few ventures into contemporary interests.[20]

Special courses for teachers were listed in seventeen of the fifty colleges included in Table I. Courses designed to give aid to all from sophomore to senior who view themselves as prospective teachers of English are listed in Table II. From the entries under "Content of Course," it may be inferred that students in these courses have opportunity again to review the "classics" which served them as college entrance requirements or gave them "credits" in high school.[21]

One might conclude that, from all this desirable and extensive study of English literature, one outcome for teachers of English might be possession of a special literary vocabulary. Some special technique, however, is needed to discover, for example, whether the reading of *Hamlet* once or seven times results in

---

[19] From three hundred college catalogues arranged alphabetically within a geographical grouping by states, every sixth catalogue was taken.
[20] It is interesting to compare these returns with Tables I and II in Henry A. Burd's "English Literature Courses in the Small College" in *The English Journal*, Feb., 1914, and with A. H. R. Fairchild's "The Sequence of Courses for College and University Students Who Choose English as a Major Subject," in *The English Journal*, March, 1923.
[21] Noble, Stuart G. "The Duplication of Elementary and Secondary Subject-Matter in College English." *The English Journal*, Jan., 1923, Table I, p. 64.

8 Tests of Literary Vocabulary for Teachers of English

TABLE I
THE KIND AND EXTENT OF COURSES IN LITERATURE FOUND

[Table I: A large matrix showing 50 colleges (rows) cross-tabulated against courses in literature (columns). Column headings, left to right: American Literature, Shakespeare, Drama, English Novel, Chaucer, Survey Course, History of English Lit., Milton, Romanticism, Victorian Prose, Eighteenth Century Prose, Victorian Poetry, Development of Eng. Drama, Nineteenth Century Prose, Teachers' Course, Literary Criticism, Browning, Literature of the Bible, Tennyson and Browning, Contemporary Poetry, Nineteenth Century Poetry, Poetry, English Literature, Wordsworth, Modern Drama, Short Story, English Essay, Medieval Lit. in English, Modern Novel, Folk Lore and Ballad, American Poetry, Beowulf, Arthurian Legends, Elizabethan Literature, Modern Essay, Early English Literature, Tennyson, Eighteenth Century Poetry, Eng. and American Essays. Column totals at bottom: 45, 42, 35, 31, 27, 26, 23, 23, 22, 22, 21, 19, 17, 17, 17, 16, 13, 13, 13, 13, 12, 12, 11, 11, 10, 10, 9, 9, 9, 8, 8, 7, 6, 6, 6, 6, 6, 5, 5.]

The Importance of Vocabulary & Literary Background

IN A CHANCE SELECTION OF FIFTY COLLEGE CATALOGUES

Course	Total
Pre-Elizabethan Literature	16
Masterpieces of Eng. Lit.	9
Contemporary Fiction	5
Biography	12
Dante in English	14
Eng. Lit. of the Renaissance	33
Development of Fiction	11
American Fiction	11
Modern Poetry	16
Romantic Poets	11
Literature of the World	10
American Prose	17
Seventeenth Century Poetry	8
Nineteenth Century Fiction	19
Contemporary Literature	15
Modern Poets	7
Old English Literature	15
Greek Lit. in Eng. Trans.	13
Sonnets of Shakespeare	0
Elizabethan Drama	11
English and American Literature	15
British Fiction	9
American Essay	5
Matthew Arnold	4
Lincoln's Writings	13
Alfredian Prose	12
Celtic Literature in English	22
Elizabethan Research	9
Pastoral Poetry	7
State Literature	9
Tudor-Stuart Drama	14
Travel Literature	9
Scott	23
Burke	16
English Poetry and Philosophy	29
Eighteenth Century Essay	12
English Letters	27
Tragedy	17
Kipling	29
Emerson's Essays	10
Contemporary Prose	14
Classics in Translation	28
	10
	13
	23
	12
	17
	19
	10
	12

10 *Tests of Literary Vocabulary for Teachers of English*

TABLE II

SEVENTEEN TEACHERS' COURSES IN ENGLISH FOUND IN A CHANCE SELECTION OF FIFTY COLLEGES

THE NUMBERS CORRESPOND TO THE NUMBERS OF THE COLLEGES LISTED IN TABLE I.

College	Title of Course	Number of Semesters	Credit	Pre-requisite	Department Credit	Content	To Whom Open
6	Teachers' Course	1	2			Lectures, reading, and conference on teaching of English in secondary schools	Seniors and graduates who intend to teach English
7	Methods of Teaching English in High School	1	2		May be counted on education credits by English majors	Principles and methods of teaching grammar, composition and the various types of literature in the junior and senior high school	Students above Freshman class
8	Teachers' Course in English	1	2 to 3			This course is especially adapted to those who are preparing themselves for high-school teaching	
9	Teachers' Course	1	2				Open to all but Freshmen
12	Teaching of English	2	2	English Composition; History of English Literature; American Literature		Methods of teaching English in the public schools	Recommended to students taking English as a major with expectation of teaching it
14	Secondary Education: Methods in Secondary English					In this course a study is made of selections from the literature that is suitable for the secondary school. Attention is given to the correlation of the study of literature and the work in composition. Special emphasis is placed upon plans for the motivation of all secondary English work	Juniors before practice teaching

The Importance of Vocabulary & Literary Background

TABLE II (Continued)

The numbers correspond to the numbers of the colleges listed in Table I.

College	Title of Course	Number of Semesters	Credit	Pre-requisite	Department Credit	Content	To Whom Open
15	Teachers' Training Course	2	3			This course is designed to prepare students to teach English composition and English literature in secondary schools	Only to seniors
17	The Teaching of English	1	3	Composition, two semesters. Types of literature two semesters	Same as Ed. 64	This course includes the study from the point of view of the classroom of a large number of the masterpieces generally read in the high school	
27	Methods of Teaching the English Classics and Composition in junior and senior high school	2	2				To juniors and seniors
28	Methods of teaching English	1	2	Old and Middle English required of those who are to be recommended as teachers of English			
30	Methods of teaching English in secondary schools	1	2	Principles of Education, Principles and Methods of Secondary Education, Anglo-Saxon, or History of English Language, Methods of Teaching spoken English, Comparative Phonetics, Vocal Interpretation of Literature		Methods of teaching the high school English required by the Association of Colleges and Preparatory Schools of the Middle States and Maryland	Optional to seniors taking English minor or equivalent who are recommended by head of department

12 Tests of Literary Vocabulary for Teachers of English

TABLE II (Concluded)
THE NUMBERS CORRESPOND TO THE NUMBERS OF THE COLLEGES LISTED IN TABLE I.

College	Title of Course	Number of Semesters	Credit	Pre-requisite	Department Credit	Content	To Whom Open
31	English for Teachers	1	2			Study of problems and methods in the teaching of composition and literature in the high school	Prospective teachers of English
32	Teachers' Course	1	3		May apply on education credit for state teaching certificate	This course is designed for students who are pursuing courses leading to a major in English and who are planning to teach the subject in the high school	Seniors and juniors who have completed fifteen hours of English
35	Teachers' Course in English	2	3			A study of principles and methods with special reference to secondary schools: (a) Composition (b) Literature	
37	Teaching of English Literature			Ten hours of English junior standing			
42	The Teaching of English in the Secondary School	1	2		Listed as both Education and English		Primarily for juniors and seniors
46	The Teaching of English Literature	1	2				

"grasping a word (*arras, fardels, orisons, gyves*) in its meaning and thereby performing an act of intelligent selection or analysis and widening the fund of meanings or concepts readily available in further intellectual enterprises." [22] At present there is available no perfected technique to discover whether the reading of

[22] Dewey, *op. cit.*, p. 180.

certain types of literature results in the acquisition of a vocabulary which seems to indicate acquaintance with specific sources; as yet there is no way of proving definitely that knowing certain words does indicate familiarity with certain types and ranges of reading. Until these questions can be answered on the basis of experimental knowledge, it seems admissible, in attempting to measure the literary vocabulary of teachers of English, to draw specific source materials of tests from the special fields of English literature which teachers of English have had the same, or at least ample, opportunity for knowing.

CHAPTER II

THE MAKING OF THE TESTS

THE BASIS OF CHOICE

The two hundred words, which make up the two literary vocabulary tests for teachers of English presented in this study, have been drawn largely from the special fields of English literature, the concern of teachers of English both in study and in teaching. Certain considerations governed the choice of words which were considered suitable for literary word knowledge tests. Obviously, random samplings from a dictionary would fail to yield a specialized English literary vocabulary; an exhaustive word count involving purely literary material was not possible within the limits of time and energy available. No definite attempt was made to select words on the basis of the number of times they appeared in the works of one author, or of many. Certainly the wanderings of *arras, meed, argent,* and *ruth* could be traced from Spenser, through Shakespeare to Shelley, and the journeys of *gest, hind,* and *byre* could be mapped from the songs of the traditional ballad singer to reminiscent echoes in modern book titles or headings for a department in a magazine. The considerations which did enter into the choice of words for the tests were one or more of the following, with the choices preferably made from sources commonly used in English classes in secondary schools.

1. Occurrence in a supposedly familiar or famous passage of English prose or poetry.

2. Occurrence in prose or poetry of a certain historical period included in the special field of English literature.

3. Occurrence in specific passages of prose or poetry, in addition to association with special periods of history, or with certain modes of religious and secular living and thinking which have become a part of English literary background, as well as a part of the general social inheritance.

4. Occurrence in the so-called technical vocabulary of names of types of literature, figures of speech, critical terms and the like, in addition to occurrence in general literature.

Examples of words chosen in accordance with the first consideration are *gowan*, which occurs in the familiar "Annie Laurie," "like dew on the gowan lying"; *jo*, in "John Anderson, my jo"; and *braes*, in "Flow gently, sweet Afton, among thy green braes." Examples from a famous passage are the italicized words in these lines taken from the soliloquy of Hamlet beginning, "To be or not to be."

> When he himself might his *quietus* make
> With a bare bodkin? Who would these *fardels* bear
> To grunt and sweat under a weary life,
> But that the dread of something after death,
> The undiscovered country from whose *bourn*
> No traveller returns, puzzles the will,
>
> . . . .
>
> The fair Ophelia! Nymph, in thy *orisons*
> Be all my sins remembered.

Under the second heading, occurrence in prose or poetry of a certain period or author, come words like *cynosure* and *dight* from Milton's "L'Allegro"; *spate, basilisk,* and *boon* from Tennyson's *Idylls of the King;* and *arras, argosy,* and *gyve* from Shakespeare.

Many words which occur in specific passages of prose and poetry carry an added weight of association with special periods or events of history, as, for example, *sansculotte* with the French Revolution and *hegira* with the flight of Mohammed; the whole history of chivalry is associated with words like *panoply, liege, largesse, seneschal, paynim, paladin, pricking.* The English Bible is inseparably linked with *jeremiad, phylactery,* and *shibboleth;* the history and the service of the church are associated with *sacerdotal, anchorite, palmer,* and *matins, liturgy, missal,* and *canticle.* In this same group are words like *hecatomb, dithyramb,* and *bacchanal,* which recall other worships and other gods; *nirvana* and *wassail, sibylline,* and *minnesinger,* each of which is an epitome of human behavior under varying conditions.

Examples of words considered a part of the technical vocabulary of English are *analogy, genre, gloss, aphorism.*

THE TEST FORM

The test form chosen for the construction of the two vocabulary tests is the selection form used in the Thorndike Tests of Word Knowledge. Five options are given from which to choose the word which most nearly means the same as the test word at the beginning of each line. Thorndike, in commenting on the selection form of test, says that it "tends to represent a rather vague, inadequate, and loose knowledge, but it can be made to represent a very exacting standard, as when fine distinctions are required or temptations to error are introduced."[1] These suggestions were adopted, and the endeavour was made to provide options which present certain problems in association, spelling, and pronunciation. Specific ways in which "temptations to error" were introduced were by opposites, by definitions of words of similar sound or spelling, and by inclusions of "high-sounding", but essentially meaningless terms. Whenever it was possible the options were chosen from the same kinds of words—ships, weapons, poetical terms—in order to make the choice more difficult. So far as it could be done the vocabulary of the options was kept on a general literary level.

These examples of test words with their accompanying options illustrate some of the temptations to error. The words in parenthesis following the options are suggestive of misleading associations; the correct response is italicized.

basilisk —oblong hall (shape of basilica); fortress (bastille); *fabulous reptile;* head piece (basinet); early church (basilica)

lamia —priest (lama); small camel (llama); fairies' child; elegy (lament); *snake woman*

nomad —bereaved woman (Niobe); sportsman (nimrod); wise old man (nestor); adviser; *wanderer*

incarnadine —imprison (incarcerate); *crimson;* embody (incarnate); urge (incite); bespatter

necromancy —death roll (necrology); mortification of bones (necrosis); undue favor (nepotism); *magic;* coining new words (neology)

picaroon —bull-fighter (picador); outcast (pariah); *rogue;* pantomime character (pantaloon); trifle (picayune)

quinquereme—church holiday (quinquagesima); refined extract (quintessence); five-sided (five banks of oars); cinchona bark (quinine); *ancient galley*

[1] Thorndike, Edward L. *Vocabularies of School Pupils.* Contributions to Education, New York Society for the Experimental Study of Education, Vol. I, p. 74.

The Making of the Tests

These are examples of test words with options which involve a choice between the same or related types of things or persons. The correct response is italicized.

argosy—phantom ship fabulous navy *merchant vessel* slave galley war vessel
anchorite—novice *hermit* priestess votary convert
harquebus—long bow *portable gun* battering ram dart blunt spear
scrannel pipes—oaten stop *reedy pipes* bag pipes haunted pipes pipes of Pan
buskin—comedy roaring farce clog dance pageantry *tragedy*

The experimental arrangement of the words, selected in accordance with the considerations of choice previously explained, in the two forms [2] of the word knowledge test, L_1 and L_2, is in a cycle of seven with this order of recurrence in the sources:

I. Ballads, songs, familiar speech
II. Technical terms
III. Familiar poetical passages
IV. Special periods, literary backgrounds
V. Special periods, literary backgrounds
VI. General literature
VII. Shakespeare

With this order of recurrence throughout the one hundred words in each form, there are available approximately fourteen words from each type of source, if one form only is used, and twenty-eight approximately when both forms are used. The particular advantage of this type of experimental arrangement is that it gives a convenient check, useful for special diagnosis, on the types or periods of literature in which vocabulary may be lacking.

The specific literary sources of the words arranged under the numbers of the sources, I, II, III, and so on, are given in Appendix B. They are individually numbered to correspond to their numbers in the experimental test forms, L_1 and L_2. The bibliographies for these sources are given separately for the two experimental forms of the test, and are marked to indicate the use made of the various sources in English courses in secondary

[2] For the experimental arrangement of the test forms, L_1 and L_2, see Appendix A.

schools, and to indicate duplications of titles in high school and college English courses.

CHARACTERIZATION OF TEST GROUPS

The tests, L_1 and L_2, were given to class groups, principally, with no definite time limit for completion, since the primary object of the tests was not speed but extent of vocabulary.[3]

The time consumed by individuals taking the tests varied from fifteen minutes to thirty minutes for each form. The persons taking the tests were asked to underline on the test forms the items which represented their academic equipment for English teaching, the type of position that they had most recently held in the field of English teaching, and to record the number of years that they had taught English of any particular rank. The results of the information gained from this source appear later in the study, both in the complete tables of data in Appendix E and in the various tables.[4]

The total score in each form of the test is the number of correct responses made. In making up the tables of data from the test papers, these items appear for each case: score for L_1, score for L_2, L_{av} (the arithmetic mean of the two scores in L_1 and L_2), Degree, Position, Experience (in number of years).

Giving the tests to numbers of high school English teachers of varying ability, preparation, and experience was made possible through the courtesy of Professor Allan Abbott and Professor Franklin T. Baker of Teachers College and the coöperation of members of their classes who lent themselves to the task of discovering the extent and kind of their literary vocabularies as indicated by their scores in L_1 and L_2.

Group A in all the data is a summer session class (1924) of one hundred and fifty-five teachers and prospective teachers of English who were enrolled in a course in the teaching of literature in secondary schools. The educational backgrounds of members of this group as they are indicated by college degrees obtained, number of years of experience in English teaching, and positions held most recently at the time of taking the tests are a part of the

---

[3] In this chapter and later, L_1 means test of Literary Vocabulary Form 1, L_2 means test of Literary Vocabulary Form 2; L_{av} means the arithmetic mean of the scores in L_1 and L_2.

[4] For statistical assistance in making Tables III to VII and in calculating coefficients of correlation shown in Tables VIII to XII as well as coefficients of multiple correlation, I am grateful to Mrs. Zaida F. Miner.

tables of data given fro Group A, and for the remaining groups in Appendix E.

Group B in all the data is a summer session class (1924) of fifty-five teachers and prospective teachers of English who were enrolled in a course in the teaching of English composition in secondary schools.

Group C in all the data is a winter session class (1924) of sixty-three teachers and prospective teachers of English enrolled in a course in the teaching of composition in secondary schools.

Group D is a winter session class (1924) of fifty-six teachers and prospective teachers of English enrolled in a course in the teaching of literature in secondary schools.

Group E is composed of thirty-six English teachers, who took the English Departmental Examination (January, 1925). The members of this group had previously been members of one or the other of Groups A, B, and C. Complete records for this group were assembled separately so that they could be used more conveniently.

Group F is composed of nineteen English teachers (previously members of Groups A, B, or C) who took the English Departmental Examinations (August, 1924). This, however, was not the same examination as that taken by Group E. Their complete records were assembled from the data of the groups in which they were first listed.

Group G is a spring session class (1925) of nineteen English teachers enrolled in a course in experiment and research in the teaching of English.

Group H is composed of twenty-seven teachers of English in one of the best New York City high schools. The members of this group are teachers who have had excellent training and who have satisfied fairly exacting standards as to their general ability in the field of English. On the whole they might be considered a representative group of the best type of English teachers in respect to their academic preparation, their length of satisfactory service, and the types of positions which they now hold.

Group I is composed of forty-nine persons outside the field of special English training and teaching. In this group were eight men, college undergraduates; seventeen persons engaged in various kinds of research work and holding degrees ranging from

A. B. to Ph.D.; four persons engaged particularly in scientific work; one teacher of high school Latin; one teacher of high school mathematics; seven persons with Ph.D. degrees holding positions above the rank of college instructors in their special fields, eleven persons with A. B. degrees (not taken in English) engaged in occupations ranging from homemaker to private secretary.

TABLE III

DISTRIBUTIONS OF TEST SCORES IN L_1, L_2, AND L_{av} FOR GROUPS A TO G COMBINED AND GROUPS H AND I

A to G, $n=406$; I, $n=49$; H, $n=27$

Interval	L_1			L_2			L_{av}		
	A to G	I	H	A to G	I	H	A to G	I	H
95–99	1	2	1	1	2	1			
90–94	3	3	2	4	3	1	3	2	2
85–89	14	4	6	6	3	3	11	2	5
80–84	20	3	5	9	5	3	14	4	4
75–79	20	6	5	19	6	6	22	3	6
70–74	17	7	3	26	5	5	16	5	4
65–69	26	4	2	23	3	3	22	7	1
60–64	27	3	1	28	5	1	32	6	3
55–59	37	7		30	5	2	35	4	
50–54	34	1	1	45	5		33	4	
45–49	37	4	1	50	1	2	34	5	2
40–44	40	1		44	4		45	2	
35–39	46	4		50			50	2	
30–34	38			35	2		40	2	
25–29	22			19			22	1	
20–24	13			11			9		
15–19	6			5			6		
10–14	3			1			2		
5–9	2								
0–4									
Q^1	36.9	51.75	72.92	38.1	50.25	67.92	37.3	50.31	70.94
Q^2	49.5	65.36	80.50	48.8	64.17	75.42	48.3	63.75	77.92
Q^3	62.6	69.79	87.04	62.6	75.75	82.08	62.9	73.75	85.25
2 Q	25.7	18.04	14.12	24.5	25.50	14.16	25.6	23.44	14.31

The Making of the Tests

TABLE IV

Distributions of L_{av} Scores of Groups A to H, Combined, According to Degrees Held, and of Group I

A to H, $n=429$ I, $n=49$

Score	Nor.	–A.B.	A.B.	–A.M.	A.M.	–Ph.D.	Ph.D.	Group I
100								
95								
90			3		1			2
85		1	6		6			3
80			5	2	8			4
75	1		12	5	6	1	1	3
70		2	9	2	7			6
65			11	3	5		3	7
60		6	18	1	11		1	4
55		1	18	2	13			3
50		3	17	3	8			7
45		3	24	7	11			1
40	1	5	23	6	13			4
35	1	4	20	4	20			1
30		5	20	5	16			4
25		2	10	1	8			
20			7		4			
15			2		2			
10		1			2			
5								
0								
Total	3	33	205	41	141	1	5	49
50–100	1	13	99	18	65	1	5	39
0–49	2	20	106	23	76	0	0	10

22 Tests of Literary Vocabulary for Teachers of English

TABLE V

DISTRIBUTIONS OF L_{av} SCORES OF GROUPS OF TEACHERS OF ENGLISH ACCORDING TO YEARS OF EXPERIENCE IN TEACHING AND OF GROUP I

Teachers, $n=433$.   Group I, $n=49$.

Score	0	1	2	3	4	5	6	7	8	9	10	11	12	13	14	15	16	18	19	20	21	22	24	26	27	29	Group I
100																											
95																											
90					1						2						1										2
85	1	1						1				3	1		1			1		2					1	1	3
80	3	1			1	1				1	1	1		3	1		1			1							4
75	5	1	2	1	3		1	3	2	1				1	2	1				1		1	1				3
70	2	1	1		3	1		4	2		1	2		1						1		1					6
65	3			6	2	1			5		1	1		1								1					7
60	9	5	3	3	3	2	2	1	1	3	2	1	1	1		1								1			4
55	2	6	6	3	3		4	1	2	4		1								2							3
50	8	3	6	1	1		3		1	2	3	1				1					1	1					7
45	9	9	2	2	4	4	3	4	2	3	2	2				1											1
40	12	4	7	2	6	8	2	1	1		1	2	1			1											4
35	11	4	10	6	2	3	3	2	3		2		1			1	1		1								1
30	12	13	8	3	2	3	3	1			1																4
25	8	2	3	3	1	2	1		1																		
20	2	1		1	6						1																
15	2	1				1																					
10	3																										
5																											
0																											
Total	92	52	48	31	37	30	20	18	23	10	18	13	4	5	6	5	5	1	1	4	2	1	3	1	2	1	49
50–100	33	18	18	14	16	9	8	10	16	7	11	9	2	5	6	3	4	1	0	4	2	1	3	1	2	1	39
0–49	59	34	30	17	21	21	12	8	7	3	7	4	2	0	0	2	1	0	1	0	0	0	0	0	0	0	10

The Making of the Tests

TABLE VI

DISTRIBUTIONS OF L_{av} SCORES OF GROUPS A TO H COMBINED, ACCORDING TO POSITION, AND OF GROUP I.

A to H, $n=420$.   I, $n=49$

Score	No Experience	Junior High School Teacher	High School Teacher	Head of Department	Normal Instructor	Supervisor	College Instructor	Group I
100								
95								
90			2	2				2
85	1		8	4				3
80	2		6	4	1	1		4
75	5	1	16	3			1	3
70	2		11	5			2	6
65	3	1	9	4	1		4	7
60	7	6	15	3	2		3	4
55	2		22	6	2		2	3
50	8	2	14	5		2		7
45	8	4	26	6			1	1
40	10	6	23	1		1	5	4
35	10	6	21	7	2	1	1	1
30	11	8	19	4	1		1	4
25	7	1	10	3				
20	2		6	2		1		
15	1		2					
10	2							
5								
0								
Total	81	35	210	59	9	6	20	49
50–100	30	10	103	36	6	3	12	39
0–49	51	25	107	23	3	3	8	10

The reliability coefficient (Pearson formula) of the experimental forms of the tests L_1 and L_2 is shown for Groups A to I inclusive in Table VII. The range is from .83 ±.01 for Group G to .94 ± .02 for Group F with an average for all groups [5] of .89.

TABLE VII
Reliability Coefficient of Experimental Test Forms L_1 and L_2

Group	n	r	P.E.
A	155	.88	± .01
B	55	.93	± .01
C	63	.91	± .01
D	57	.87	± .02
E	36	.90	± .02
F	19	.94	± .02
G	19	.83	± .05
H	27	.85	± .04
I	49	.91	± .02

Distributions of test scores in L_1 and L_2, and L_{av} are given in Table III for teachers of English, groups A to G combined for the special group not teachers of English, Group I, and for Group H, a highly selected group of teachers of English. Tables IV, V, and VI show the distributions, respectively, of L_{av} scores of all groups of English teachers according to degree in English, years of experience, and position held, in contrast with the distribution of Group I. These distributions present different arrangements of the data to make somewhat clearer any relationship existing

---

[5] The scores in L_1 and L_2 for all teachers of English were put together with a total of 406 cases (duplications counted but once). As judged by $N = 406$, the r for L_1 and L_2 is .90 ± .01

By formula, $$r = \frac{2r_{L_1 L_2}}{1 + r_{L_1 L_2}}$$

the true reliability of the entire test ($L_1 + L_2$) is .95. If the reliability of one half with another half is to be made .95, the test must be twice as long. (By another form of the same formula

$$N = r \frac{1 - r_{L_1 L_2}}{r_{L_1 L_2}(1 - r)} \cdot)$$

In case the test were thus increased in length by adding one hundred more words to each half, the total reliability of the four hundred words (assuming the additional words to be of reliability equal to that of the present selection) would then be .97. (See Kelley, *Statistical Method*, Chap. VI. Formulas quoted from Spearman, 1911, and Brown, 1910.) These figures indicate, therefore, that the present tests are of adequate length and reliability for all ordinary practical usages.

between the test scores and other characteristics of the subjects taking the tests.[6]

The order of difficulty of the test words as determined by experiment is shown in the table in Appendix C in which can be found the ranks of the two hundred words in L_1 and L_2, determined by the permilles of teachers of English, and others, making correct responses to each word.

The test scores, alone, of the teachers of English and the reporting of the specific degree of difficulty for each element in the two forms of the test are useful so far as they go; the self-correlation of the two forms is satisfactory; the next step in establishing the validity of the tests is finding out what test scores mean in terms of other tests and attainments, and what the tests really measure.

[6] These scores made by persons taking both tests, L_1 and L_2, together with L_{av} are recorded in the complete tables of data given in Appendix D. The complete record for each case, including data used in Chapter III of this study, is presented in the tables for the respective groups.

In using the material from the test forms for Tables IV, V, and VI, showing the distribution of L_{av} according to "A. Degree, B. Experience, and C. Position," as well as in the computations for Chapter III, these items were considered as follows:

A. Degree (as indicating type of academic preparation in English):
  1. Normal school diploma,
  2. Work toward A.B. in English,
  3. A.B. in English (work toward B.S. in Education with English major, and B.S. in Education with English major are included under the two immediately preceeding heads),
  4. Work toward A.M. in English,
  5. A.M.,
  6. Work toward Ph.D. in English, and
  7. Ph.D. in English.

These seven groups appear in the table headings as: n, -A.B., A.B., -A.M., A.M., -Ph.D., and Ph.D.

B. Experience (number of years spent in the teaching of English) from 0 no teaching experience) by single years to twenty-nine.

C. Position (the type held at the time of taking the test, or most recently held in the field of English teaching):
  1. 0—(had held no position),
  2. Teacher in Junior High School,
  3. Teacher in High School,
  4. Head of Department,
  5. Normal Instructor,
  6. Supervisor of English (either in high school or normal school),
  7. College Instructor.

CHAPTER III

THE RELATION OF LITERARY VOCABULARY TO OTHER ATTAINMENTS

In the foregoing presentation of the tests of word knowledge specifically related to the field of English literature, with their specific sources and general settings in relation to the whole background of the study and the teaching of English, emphasis has been placed particularly on the vocabulary of the two forms of the tests, the results in terms of scores, and the order of difficulty of the words for those taking the tests. It is purposed in Chapter III to show the relation of word knowledge, in the specific field of English literature—for this study represented by the arithmetic mean of the scores of L_1 and L_2, the two tests constructed and given as experiments in the exploration of the literary word knowledge of teachers of English—to other attainments of teachers as shown by their academic preparation, their experience (in terms of years), and by certain measures of intelligence and achievement.

The groups which were used in the study of these relationships were those previously characterized on pages 18 and 19. For *Groups A, B,* and *C,* there were available the following records:

1. Scores in L_1, L_2, and L_{av}.
2. Academic degrees (taken in English).
3. Experience (in terms of years).
4. Types of English positions most recently held.

These four items were obtained from answers to questions printed on the test forms.

5. Scores in Army Alpha, Form 7.
6. Scores in Thorndike Intelligence Examination, Part III (1923).
7. Scores in North Carolina Exercises in Judging Prose. (Hereafter spoken of as Trabue Prose Judging.)

8. Semester marks in English for the single courses in connection with which the tests were given.

For *Group D,* the records were available in the four items gained from the test forms and in the semester marks in English for the single course in connection with which the tests were given.

For *Group E,* composed of English teachers who had previously been members of *Groups A, B,* or *C,* a complete assembling of records was made in the eight items listed above, with the addition of scores in an English Departmental Examination, a general examination in the field of English subject matter required by Teachers College of all candidates for a degree or a diploma in English.

For *Group F,* formed under the same conditions as *Group E,* the scores in the English Departmental Examination were available, together with complete records in other items. The Departmental Examination was not the same as that which the members of *Group E* took.

For *Group G,* the records obtained from the test forms only were available. This group appears only once, in Table VIII, on page 28.

For *Group H,* the records in the four items obtained from the test forms were used.

For *Group I,* the records included the test scores, academic degrees and type of work in which the person was engaged.

The relation of word knowledge related rather specifically to the field of English literature—in this study represented by L_{av}, the arithmetic mean of the scores for L_1 and L_2—and measures of intelligence and achievement—is shown by the correlations in Table VIII. Most teachers of English are possessed of certain qualifications in common, such as academic degrees of one kind or another [1] and experience in teaching in some type of English work. The correlation of L_{av} with degree is uniformly low: the highest .34 ± .12 for Group H (a highly selected group of teachers) and the lowest —.02 ± .15 for Group F (a small number of teachers who took one of the Departmental Examinations).

Experience in terms of years does not correlate closely with

---

[1] No attempt has been made to discover for individual cases the specific kind or quality of academic work represented by degrees; all degrees listed were accepted as equally significant or the several groupings made.

TABLE VIII
Correlation Coefficients of L_av Scores with Other Variables

Group	n	Army Alpha r	P.E.	Thorndike Intelligence III r	P.E.	Trabue Prose r	P.E.	Departmental Examination r	P.E.	English Mark r	P.E.	Degree r	P.E.	Experience r	P.E.	Position r	P.E.	Age r	P.E.
A	155	.54	±.04	.57	±.04	.49	±.04			.77	±.02	.07	±.05	.19	±.05	−.04	±.05	.18	±.07
B	55	.69	±.05	.63	±.05	.65	±.05			.72	±.05	−.04	±.09	.29	±.08	.24	±.08		
C	63	.54	±.06	.63	±.05	.32	±.08			.73	±.04	−.13	±.08	.32	±.08	.23	±.08		
D	57							.77	±.07	.30	±.08	.30	±.08	.27	±.08	.16	±.08		
E	36	.65	±.07	.68	±.06	.44	±.09	.75	±.05	.74	±.05	−.25	±.11	.29	±.10	.20	±.13		
F	19	.64	±.09	.48	±.12	.71	±.08			.77	±.06	−.02	±.12	.52	±.11	.31	±.14	.14	±.12
H	27							.88	±.03			.34		.51	±.10	.29	±.12		

TABLE IX
Correlation Coefficients of Army Alpha with Other Variables

Group	n	Departmental Examination r	P.E.	English Mark r	P.E.	Degree r	P.E.	Experience r	P.E.	Position r	P.E.	Thorndike Intelligence III r	P.E.	Trabue Prose r	P.E.
A	155			.54	±.04	−.009	±.05	.03	±.05	−.04	±.05	.61	±.03	.44	±.04
B	55			.55	±.06	−.16	±.08	.05	±.08	.09	±.08	.61	±.05	.51	±.06
C	63			.50	±.06	−.38	±.07	−.07	±.08	−.10	±.08	.67	±.04	.43	±.06
D	57			.15	±.08	−.08	±.08	.02	±.08	.22	±.08	.71	±.09		
E	36	.53	±.08	.41	±.09	−.37	±.10	−.06	±.11	−.27	±.10			.47	±.09
F	19	.77	±.06	.62	±.10	−.20	±.16	.26	±.16	.33	±.15			.72	±.08

specialized English vocabulary as it is represented by L_{av}. Again, Group H (a highly selected group of teachers from the English department of a New York high school, containing teachers with a range of experience from one to twenty-nine years) ranks highest with a correlation of .51 ± .10. Group A (a summer session class in one English course) ranks lowest, with .19 ± .05. The correlations of L_{av} with experience in teaching are, to be sure, higher than the correlations of L_{av} with degree, but they are not large enough to be indicative of significant relationship between experience and literary vocabulary as evidenced by the L_{av} scores. The type of position held correlates only a little more with L_{av} than degree correlated, and not so much as experience. For the largest, Group A, the correlation is –.04 ± .05; that of Group F is highest, .31 ± .14.

For ninety-two members of Group A and thirty-four members of Group E, chronological ages were available. The correlations of L_{av} with age, .18 ± .07 for A, and .14 ± .12 for E, reveal little correspondence between specialized literary vocabulary and the age of the teacher of English. So far as degree in English, experience in teaching, position, and age are concerned, the correlations between them and L_{av} hover persistently around zero, with the exception of one highly selected group, H, which has a correlation of .51 ± .10 with experience. Tables IX, X, and XI on pages 28 and 30 are included for purposes of comparison to show that the correlations of Army Alpha, Thorndike, and Trabue, with the same factors of degree, experience, and position exhibit the same general tendencies toward low correlations, and therefore the low correlations of L_{av} cannot be ascribed to peculiar or untoward characteristics of the literary vocabulary tests.

The correlation of word knowledge with measures of intelligence and achievement is considerably and consistently higher than the correlation with degree, experience, and position. Of the three tests used with the groups in this study, Army Alpha on the whole correlates most highly with L_{av}, with a range from .54 ± .04 and .54 ± .06 for Groups A and C, to .69 ± .05 for Group B. The correlation of L_{av} with the Thorndike Intelligence Examination, Part III, is the next highest, with a range from .48 ± .12 for Group F, to .68 ± .06 for Group G. In this examination the individual score "is a measure of intelligence

TABLE X
Correlation Coefficients of Thorndike Intelligence Examination, Part III, with Other Variables

Group	n	Departmental Examination r	P.E.	English Mark r	P.E.	Degree r	P.E.	Experience r	P.E.	Position r	P.E.	Army Alpha r	P.E.	Trabue Prose r	P.E.
A	155			.59	± .04	−.12	± .05	−.03	± .05	−.12	± .05	.61	± .03	.40	± .05
B	55			.57	± .06	−.05	± .09	.11	± .09	.05	± .09	.60	± .05	.53	± .07
C	63			.51	± .06	−.18	± .08	−.08	± .08	−.07	± .08	.67	± .04	.39	± .07
D	57											.71	± .09		
E	36	.49	± .09	.54	± .08										
F	19	.48	± .12	.29	± .16										

TABLE XI
Correlation Coefficients of Trabue Prose Judging with Other Variables

Group	n	Departmental Examination r	P.E.	English Mark r	P.E.	Degree r	P.E.	Experience r	P.E.	Position r	P.E.	Army Alpha r	P.E.	Thorndike r	P.E.
A	155			.57	± .04	−.14	± .05	.04	± .05	−.02	± .05	.44	± .04	.40	± .05
B	55			.66	± .05	−.01	± .09	.36	± .08	.24	± .09	.51	± .06	.53	± .07
C	63			.37	± .07	.005	± .08	.15	± .07	.18	± .08	.43	± .06	.39	± .07
D	57											.47	± .09		
E	36	.47	± .09									.72	± .08		
F	19	.70	± .08												

Relation of Literary Vocabulary to Other Attainments

as it operates in careful reading and study. It measures a composite of abilities of great importance for college work in History, Government, Economics, Sociology, Literature, Philosophy, and Psychology and for professional work in law, theology or education."[2] L_{av} with Trabue Prose Judging yields correlations ranging from .32 ± .08 for Group C to .65 ± .05 for Group B.

There remain the two more specific indications of achievement in English,—English mark in a single English course (the course indicated in the characterizations of the test groups) and score in the English Departmental Examination. With these, L_{av} correlates more highly consistently through the various groups. This same tendency is also noticeable in Tables IX, X, and XI, pages 28 and 30, for Army Alpha, Thorndike, and Trabue. The correlation of work knowledge in the specific field of English literature with semester English marks in a single English course is fairly high, with a range from .30 ± .08 for Group D to .77 ± .06 for Group F.

The L_{av} correlations of Groups D (only 16 members of which took the examination), E (36) and F (16) with the Departmental English Examination were, respectively, .77 ± .07, .75 ± .05, and .88 ± .03. The number of cases in these groups is small; the examination is required of those who are candidates for a degree or diploma in English in secondary schools. Not all of the persons who took the Departmental Examination had been members of the classes for which other tests and measures were available. The records of those who took this examination and who also had complete records otherwise were assembled separately and correlations made from these data. The elements entering into the examination, which was largely objective and scored by points, were mainly informal tests of literary ability or familiarity with certain facts and materials of literature, such as allusions, quotations, literary backgrounds, knowledge of authors and current books, and word knowledge.

Table XII, page 32, gives a summary, showing the average intercorrelations of L_{av} with the various factors which entered into the study of the tests, L_1 and L_2, to determine their value as shown by relationships existing between them and other tests and attainments.

[2] Thorndike, E. L. Instructions for Giving, Scoring and Interpreting Scores. Thorndike Intelligence Examination for High School Graduates. Series 1925-30.

32   Tests of Literary Vocabulary for Teachers of English

TABLE XII
Average Intercorrelations of Various Factors Considered in Word Knowledge Prognosis

	L_{av}	Army Alpha	Thorndike	Trabue
Army Alpha, Form 7	.61			
Thorndike Intelligence Examination, Part III	.60	.65		
Trabue Prose Judging	.52	.51	.44	
English Departmental Examinations	.80	.65	.48	.59
English Mark in One Course	.77	.46	.50	.53
Degree	−.01	−.20	−.12	.005
Position	.18	.18	−.04	.15
Experience	.34	.03	.00	.18
Age	.16			

WHAT THE TESTS MEASURE

Knowing the correlations of L_{av} with various qualifications and attainments of English teachers, it is of interest to know, in addition to these, the combinations of factors involved which will give the best prediction of L_{av}. For example, for Group E (thirty-six cases), the largest group for which scores in the English Departmental Examination are available, it is known that the correlations with L_{av} are .75 for Departmental Examination, .73 for semester mark in English, −.24 for degree, and .28 for experience. By using the multiple correlation procedure, it is found that the L_{av} score can be predicted to the extent of a correlation of .85 by a combination of English Departmental Examination and semester mark in English. Adding experience and degree to the composite raises the correlation but little. The addition of experience gives .853; a composite of the four factors involved gives .854. This seems to indicate that the tests measure what they purport to measure—English literary vocabulary, or some specific ability in English—as well as to emphasize previously found low correlations of specific knowledge of literary vocabulary, as shown by L_{av}, with degree and experience.

On the correlations of semester mark in English with L_{av}, Army Alpha, Thorndike Intelligence Examination, Part III, and Trabue Prose Judging, the multiple correlation technique was used to discover the combination of these factors which will give the best measure of semester mark in English and of the English Departmental Examination. Group A, one hundred and fifty-five cases with complete records, was used in this procedure. Semester mark in English can be predicted to the extent of a correlation of .80 by L_{av} and the Trabue Measure of Ability in Judging Prose. L_{av} has the highest individual correlation, .76. The addition of the Thorndike Intelligence Examination, Part III, to L_{av}, and Trabue raises the correlation to .81. Army Alpha adds nothing significant, since a composite of L_{av}, Trabue, Thorndike, and Army Alpha predicts to the extent of a correlation of .813, as against .80 for the combination of L_{av} and Trabue Prose Judging.

L_{av} and Army Alpha combined yield the best measure of prediction for the English Departmental Examination. L_{av} has the highest individual correlation with the English Departmental Examination, .75. L_{av} and Army Alpha combined predict the Departmental Examination to the extent of a correlation of .765. Trabue Prose Judging added to the composite raises the correlation to .769. The Thorndike Intelligence Examination, Part III, adds nothing.

The best single prediction for both semester mark in English and English Departmental Examination can be made on the basis of L_{av} which correlates, respectively, .76 and .75 with such English achievements.

The best combinations for the English Departmental Examination are:

L_{av}	.76
L_{av} + Trabue Prose Judging	.80
L_{av} + Trabue + Thorndike Intelligence Examination, Part III	.81

The best combinations for the English Departmental Examination are:

L_{av}	.75
L_{av} + Army Alpha, Form 7	.77

CHAPTER IV

CONCLUSIONS

The results of this study, primarily undertaken to devise and standardize for teachers of English vocabulary tests drawn from specific literary sources, answer in some measure the questions: What kind and amount of word knowledge related rather specifically to the field of English literature is the possession of teachers of English? What relation exists between word knowledge related rather specifically to the field of English literature and other attainments of teachers of English?

The amount of such knowledge possessed by teachers of English in terms of the tests L_1 and L_2 is in individual cases sometimes very small. The median score in terms of number of words correct per one hundred in L_1 is 49; in L_2, 48; and for the arithmetic mean of the two, L_{av}, 48. Inability to make higher scores may have been due to several causes: carelessness and vagueness generally; a lack of inquisitive or acquisitive feeling for words in specific contexts; a limited range of experience; or certain disabilities with respect to sight and hearing which appear in difficulties in reading and spelling.

The tables in Appendix C, showing the order of difficulty of the test words, bear witness to both the kind and the amount of literary word knowledge (as represented in the two hundred words of L_1 and L_2) possessed by teachers of English. These tables show the comparative difficulty of words for teachers of English and for those outside that special field and perform the definite service of showing the actual order of difficulty of these words for over four hundred teachers of English.

The correlations between word knowledge specifically related to the field of English and measures of intelligence or achievement are consistently high enough to be significant, and tend to substantiate the general notion that vocabulary correlates with intelligence and with school achievements. The correlation of .60 between the arithmetic mean of the scores of the two test

Conclusions

forms, L_{av}, and the Thorndike Intelligence Examination, Part III, the individual score in which is a measure of intelligence as it operates in careful reading and study, may to that extent be indicative of the same abilities involved in the acquisition of word knowledge related to the particular field of English literature. The correlation of .52 between literary word knowledge (L_{av}) and Trabue Prose Judging may indicate that attending to words in a particular sense is to that extent measured by L_{av}.

The relatively high correlations, .80 and .67, respectively, of the specific English vocabulary of the tests and the English Departmental Examination and the semester mark in one course in English seem to indicate that the two tests of word knowledge presented in this study are fairly good measures of knowledge of English subject matter, at least of that required for the Departmental Examination and specific courses in English. This indication is further substantiated by a correlation of .85, the extent to which L_{av} can be predicted by a combination of semester mark in English and the English Departmental Examination.

The correlations of word knowledge related specifically to the field of English (L_{av}) and academic preparation (in terms of degrees in English), years of experience spent in teaching English, and present teaching position are so consistently low as to be negligible. There is apparently no appreciable correspondence between vocabulary related to the special field of English literature and degree (in English), position, and experience, which are often considered in themselves significant evidences of intelligence, attainment, and teaching ability.

The tests L_1 and L_2 are of adequate length and reliability for all ordinary practical usages. The self-correlation of the two forms is high; they have a fairly high correlation with the special knowledge of English subject matter necessary for the achievement of semester mark in English and for passing the English Departmental Examination. Since they also measure intelligence (as it operates in certain functions) to the extent of respective correlations of .60 with Thorndike Intelligence Examination, Part III, and .61 with Army Alpha, Form 7, they might conveniently and safely enough be used as a part of a selective test for prospective teachers of English.

The particular value of tests L_1 and L_2 lies in their usefulness as a measure of English achievement, particularly as that enters into semester marks in English and English Departmental Examinations. Of the tests and other measures of attainment used in this study, they provide the best single measure of prediction of success in semester marks in English and the English Departmental Examination. This prediction can be made in half an hour's time, or less, on objectively scored tests, to the extent of a correlation of .76 for semester mark in English, and one of .75 for the English Departmental Examination (which takes ordinarily three hours).

The best combination for the prediction of semester mark in English is a composite of L_{av}, Trabue Prose Judging, and the Thorndike Intelligence Examination, Part III, which predicts success to the extent of a correlation of .81. For the English Departmental Examination, the best combination is L_{av}, and Army Alpha, Form 7, a composite which yields a prediction of success to the extent indicated by a correlation of .77. The tests, then, singly or as part of a composite, offer possibilities of service as diagnostic measures, as selective measures, and as substitutes or verifying checks for longer and more formal tests of knowledge in the field of English literature as it is related to the teaching of English. The tests afford, in addition, ample opportunity for the discovery of specific individual weaknesses of vocabulary in various periods and types of literature. They should be useful particularly in teachers' colleges or in special courses for teachers of English in colleges generally, as one means of testing and classifying. They suggest themselves as a means of eliminating poorly prepared students from the ranks of prospective teachers.

Further research is needed to discover whether word knowledge in other specialized fields, such as history, is correlated with intelligence and special knowledge of that field; and to discover the correlation between the extent of word knowledge of a special field, such as English or history, and high intelligence and special ability in that field.

It would be helpful and informing, perhaps, to undertake further studies of literary vocabulary to discover the correlation between such word knowledge and the use of language as conditioning thought and expression; and to discover the relation of such word knowledge to the actual teaching skill and ability of teachers of English.

APPENDIX A

THE EXPERIMENTAL FORMS OF TESTS L_1 AND L_2

TEST OF WORD KNOWLEDGE

FORM L_1

Name .... Address.............................

Underline *all* the items which represent your equipment for high school English teaching: normal school diploma; now working toward A.B. in English; now working toward B.S. in Education with English major; A.B. in English; B.S. in Education with English major; A.M. in English; Ph.D. in English; no college electives in English.

Underline the type of position you now hold or have most recently held in the field of English teaching: junior high school teacher; junior high school supervisor; high school teacher; head of high school department; high school supervisor; normal school teacher; normal school supervisor; college instructor; head of college department.

How many years have you taught English of junior high school rank? .... of high school rank? .... of normal school rank? .... of college rank? ....

Underline the word in each line which most nearly means the same as the first word:

1. gowan — ash, daisies, blossom, meadow, grass
2. threnody — recollection, dirge, paean, wood-note, interlude
3. cates — dainties, fruits, secrets, augury, celebrations
4. paynim — river god, nymph, pagan, massacre, wizard
5. caravel — carved stone, camel train, inn, fast ship, folk song

6. avatar — evil, confession, heathen, idol, incarnation
7. fardel — burden, sticks, sword, dance, mockery
8. carl — hangman, peasant, page, sorrow, savage
9. gloss — edition, print, interpretation, mystery, stanza
10. sedge — margin, sigh, lake, border, rush

11. paladin — pleasure, mountebank, security, knight-errant, fame
12. oriflamme — incantation, inquisition, old ship, vestment, rallying point
13. saga — legend, epoch, mead, hero, inscription
14. arras — tincture, tapestry, hazard, imposing series, heraldic insignia
15. leal — land, song, distance, faithful, balm

16. bucolic — urban, sophisticated, romantic, bovine, pastoral
17. burgeon — bud, merchant, generosity, gavotte, nosegay
18. basilisk — oblong hall, fabulous reptile, head piece, fortress, early church
19. sansculotte — anarchist, supreme council, extreme republican, sacred language, socialist
20. bruit — strength, stress, shield, rumor, potion

21.	orison	ornament, constellation, vow, lamentation, prayer
22.	gest	romance, idle tale, novel, lyric form, chapter
23.	shibboleth	foreigner, watchword, weapon, seventh year, cudgel
24.	lucent	crescent, silver, shining, wooded, soothing
25.	jongleur	pale yellow, stupid person, clown, itinerant minstrel, fool
26.	hecatomb	set of seven, armorial bearings, contrary opinion, secret symbol, public sacrifice
27.	mummer	actor, hired ruffian, ceremonial, yellow cloth, dumb show
28.	springes	small game, snares, curves, billets of wood, pouches
29.	corbie	fairy, charm, raven, large basket, pet lamb
30.	epitome	age, addition, praise, summary, qualification
31.	lamia	priest, small camel, fairies' child, elegy, snake woman
32.	largesse	household deity, card game, heresy, benefice, bestowal
33.	sacerdotal	canonical, spiritual, penitential, priestly, sugarlike
34.	aegis	eternity, protection, eagle's nest, temple, magistrate
35.	gyve	spiral, spite, shackle, convolution, ridicule
36.	brae	grief, hillside, stream, bonny, dew
37.	apocryphal	uncanonical, visionary, annotated, orthodox, prophetic
38.	orient	precious, dull, iridescent, sweet, bright
39.	gammer	chatter, old woman, nonsense, brawl, hoax
40.	amulet	evil, sacred vessel, charm, precious stone, badge
41.	matins	wooden shoes, moulds, birds, morning prayer, afternoons
42.	arrant	knavish, embroidered, overbearing, deceitful, notorious
43.	burn	small stream, cottage, stall, shelter, thick woods
44.	jeremiad	prophecy, lamentation, long poem, taunt, fustian
45.	obloquy	disregard, forgetfulness, abuse, penitence, offering
46.	tabor	garment, flute, whirling dance, small drum, cup
47.	palmer	magician, minstrel, hawker, unbeliever, pilgrim
48.	anathema	blessing of church, ancient relics, responsive singing, baptism of fire, accursed thing
49.	cozen	protest, relate, bargain, cheat, comfort
50.	carline	evil eye, witch, old woman, precious stone, fabled monster
51.	dithyramb	satire, choric hymn, comic verse, balladry, meter
52.	rue	repent, abandon, despair, stain, destroy
53.	salmagundi	memoirs, miscellany, expurgated edition, obeisance, lizard
54.	beldam	reigning beauty, lunatic, ugly old woman, gipsy, drug
55.	bacchanal	card game, raillery, trifle, drunken reveller, beacon
56.	caitiff	Mohammedan ruler, street hawker, camel driver, bully, coward
57.	fain	glad, idle, priest, doom, worship
58.	vernacular	improper, mother tongue, borrowed, bi-lingual, Latin
59.	asphodel	bituminous substance, occult influence, immortal flower, emanation, literary club
60.	gargoyle	giant, braggart, mounted soldier, grotesque spout, spirit
61.	flagellate	communicate by signals, play flute, pillage, glide, scourge
62.	fortuitous	rigorous, courageous, accidental, designed, decisive
63.	bourn	blank shield, deadly sin, reward, undiscovered country, boundary
64.	byre	funeral, cottage, dove cote, cow house, sheep fold
65.	analogy	separation, fable, romance, resemblance, logic
66.	dight	speared, doubled, patterned, hoped, arrayed
67.	nomad	bereaved woman, sportsman, wise old man, adviser, wanderer
68.	hospice	pledge, stable man, charity, house of rest, mean dwelling
69.	antiphonal	hymnal, religious, responsive, clerical, thoughtful
70.	incarnadine	imprison, crimson, embody, urge, bespatter

Appendix A

71. canny — faithless, stingy, shrewd, queer, silent
72. genre — style, color, introduction, comparison, tone
73. kith — knapsack, old cat, relatives, cousin, acquaintance
74. panoply — covered basket, suit of armor, broad comedy, tourney, triumph
75. argosy — phantom ship, fabulous navy, merchant vessel, slave-galley, war vessel
76. cabal — oral tradition, occult lore, hiding place, secret intrigue, false report
77. avouch — guarantee, betrayal, confession, retribution, assertion
78. wist — desired, heeded, knew, willed, silenced
79. aphorism — example, maxim, dullness, prolixity, triteness
80. palfrey — war horse, safeguard, cloak, saddle horse, discussion
81. philistine — temperate, benevolent, uncultured, trifling, choice
82. anchorite — novice, hermit, priestess, votary, convert
83. connotation — margin, exactness, creation, implication, interlinear
84. bauble — gibe, jargon, petty quarrel, empty boast, showy trinket
85. rede — solve, puzzle, riddle, balance, thatch
86. lexicon — law book, dictionary, connection, law of retaliation, system
87. immolate — perpetuate, transfix, sacrifice, disparage, disdain
88. barrow — marshy plain, slave enclosure, grave mound, farmyard, monument
89. liturgy — apathy, oblivion, law suit, form of worship, polite learning
90. necromancy — death roll, mortification of bones, undue favor, magic, coining new words
91. thorp — brook, market place, hedge wall, village, squires' court
92. pricking — charging with spear, advancing on horse-back, cursing, joining in tourney, breaking vows
93. quair — book, garland, case for arrows, literary gossip, minutia
94. ruth — cruelty, revenge, pity, distress, fatality
95. scrip — indulgence, monk's vows, pilgrim's bag, holy relics, traveller's map
96. savant — book binding, morocco, translator, man of learning, magician
97. rubric — mystic, druid, priestly, folk-lore, direction
98. madrigal — part song, bird, morning, serenade, salutation
99. jo — jug, laddie, husband, sweetheart, sailor
100. epithet — inscription, oath, elegy, classic, appellation

TEST OF WORD KNOWLEDGE

FORM L₂

Underline the word in each line which most nearly means the same as the first word:

1. cleped — clad, hurried, called, told, cut
2. homily — exhortation, unpleasantness, proverb, inheritance, impromptu
3. rathe — brimming full, smoky, blooming early, guardian, yellow
4. myrmidon — great number, incense, sorcery, hired ruffian, Russian peasant
5. chapman — fishmonger, customer, fat-faced person, beggar, pedlar
6. utopian — visionary, socialistic, practical, subjective, valuable
7. murrain — mist, plague, marsh, debris, dry wind

Appendix

8.	kye	lea, meadow, deer, cows, border
9.	eclogue	recurring name, conclusion, pastoral dialogue, fancy, sonnet octave
10.	spate	fish eggs, mineral springs, broad road, winged monster, river flood
11.	nirvana	Buddhist beatitude, pagan philosophy, Chinese wisdom, stoicism, transmigration
12.	harlequin	pantaloon, buffoon, pantomime, hedge priest, tragic piece
13.	tutelar	tempting, pompous, protective, savage, supernatural
14.	prate	meddle, treat with magic, equalize, chatter, commend
15.	warlock	utter standstill, sentinel, jailer, watchman, sorcerer
16.	argot	mystery, dictation, style, feeling, class jargon
17.	bole	turnkey, sham, morass, stem, closed bud
18.	phylactery	tribal division, invective, amulet, stamp collecting, cleansing agent
19.	barcarole	outer defense, song of gondolier, lullaby, narrow flag, rampart
20.	apotheosis	deification, abandonment of faith, hidden writings, revelation, materialization
21.	grisly	immature, terrible, fierce, spiteful, gray-bearded
22.	hind	page, swine herd, rustic, rogue, sneak
23.	bibliophile	library, list of books, lover of books, annotation, edition
24.	coign	dagger, wimple, armor, corner, superiority
25.	leprechaun	prehistoric animal, mushroom, tomb, person with leprosy, sprite
26.	apocalypse	revelation, ascension, terse saying, secret rites, lament
27.	nadir	wealthy official, lowest point, horizon, balsam, beak
28.	avaunt	farewell, hail, begone, cease, welcome
29.	fey	cheerful, deceitful, elf-like, doomed, imaginary
30.	apologue	banality, enigma, foreword, synonym, moral fable
31.	savannah	frozen marsh, morass, coral island, high plateau, treeless plain
32.	catacomb	violated shrines, cosmic upheaval, heathen temples, disaster, underground cemeteries
33.	tabard	outer coat, brindled cat, sheath, ark, pinnacle
34.	mordant	unwholesome, caustic, at point of death, sullen, depressed
35.	usance	argument, fetish, interest, artifice, obligation
36.	corages	hearts, carrion crows, wicker boats, beaks, plumage
37.	euphuism	angling, affectation, liturgy, description, flattery
38.	timbrel	kettledrum, guillotine, tambourine, cart, vibration
39.	caravansary	covered carriage, house on wheels, Eastern inn, early hospital, asylum
40.	selah	peace, so be it, sacred enclosure, unknown meaning, grace
41.	ruck	tumult, brawl, feint, groove, crowd
42.	posset	pet lamb, peep-show, back gate, hot drink, tribal feast
43.	wight	coral reef, bark hut, person, wild duck, changeling
44.	elegy	rural, requiem, praise, heroic verse, diatribe
45.	casque	helmet, small island, lance, precious box, shield
46.	berserk	Italian sharp shooter, Norse warrior, crusading knight, free-booter, wandering poet
47.	wassail	loss by waste, drinking bout, squander, street Arab, waits' singing
48.	anodyne	positive pole, paradox, abnormality, soothing drug, response
49.	liege	ballad, tribute money, sappers' battle, feudal superior, king's ransom
50.	irk	anger, weary, condemn, inlay, confuse

Appendix A 41

51. missal — scroll, anthology, lawbook, book of devotions, appendix
52. ingle — beacon fire, thatched cottage, fire on hearth, family circle, settle
53. arbalest — sea bird, crossbow, short gun, stout club, falcon
54. bethel — abomination, house of mercy, pilgrimage, birth-right, hallowed spot
55. buskin — comedy, roaring farce, tragedy, clog dance, pageantry
56. sooth — truth, loyalty, satiety, diviner, flattery
57. minion — dwarf, favorite, mimic, bribe, dance figure
58. vignette — local color, atmosphere, sketch, analysis, marginal note
59. cynosure — young swan, cure of souls, guiding star, fault finding, recurring cycle
60. sibylline — hissing, mediæval, misleading, oracular, inspired
61. kermis — peasants' dance, burghers' council, funeral rites, fair, fermented milk
62. apogee — old maxim, highest point, sham, self-indulgence, vindication
63. indenture — coast line, compensation, improper proceeding, increase, sealed agreement
64. benison — grief, blessing, curse, vespers, chimes
65. apothegm — animal story, moral, pithy saying, allegory, figure
66. argent — silver, variegated, crescent, luxuriant, green
67. hegira — shrine, flight, pilgrimage, sacrifice, contemplation
68. genie — clan, demon, young falcon, effigy, image
69. cavil — unappreciated good, just praise, captious objection, reproof, warning
70. ravin — spoil, delirium, ill omen, wound, skein
71. fen — feudal benefice, wooded slope, open country, marsh, heather
72. strophe — address, literal reading, punishment, verse unit, riddle
73. livid — graphic, red, bright, dazzling, leaden
74. minnesinger — wayfaring fool, juggler, merry andrew, lyric poet, epic poet
75. kismet — destiny, mysticism, talisman, sweetmeat, drowsy state
76. arcana — series of arches, mysteries, antiquities, thieves' slang, ancient records
77. quietus — passive attitude, silent devotion, final riddance, disguise, deep silence
78. nonce — old lantern, socket of candle stick, indefinite future, time being, make believe
79. epigram — inscription on stone, motto, pointed saying, transitory, letter
80. boon — pennon, request, patent, duty, equipment
81. palimpsest — twilight, paints, scroll, illumination, manuscript
82. picaroon — bull-fighter, outcast, rogue, pantomime character, trifle
83. contumacious — reproachful, disgraceful, insubordinate, stubborn, quarrelsome
84. palter — linger, cheat, equivocate, tremble, recant
85. fell — veiled, sudden, unrelenting, destructive, bestead
86. pandect — ultimatum, apology, peroration, scrivener, compendium
87. meed — merited portion, honeyed words, high plain, laurel wreath, labyrinth
88. harquebus — long bow, portable gun, battering ram, dart, blunt spear
89. seneschal — yeoman, man at arms, steward, drawbridge, vassal
90. predilection — foreordination, fate, motive, prophecy, partiality
91. eke — alas, however, truly, also, no doubt
92. shawes — fields, woods, flowers, arrows, shields

Appendix

93. canticle — little song, accompaniment, order of service, revelry, rousing chorus
94. scrannel pipes — oaten stop, reedy pipes, bag pipes, haunted pipes, pipes of Pan
95. galleon — narrow hall, gold braid, drudge, Spanish vessel, oblong tray
96. quinquereme — church holiday, refined extract, five-sided, cinchona bark, ancient galley
97. arabesque — subtle, fine horse, fresco, fabulous, fantastic
98. amerce — fine, absolve, abandon, reward, hire
99. hap — handicap, tragic outcome, lot, extra weight, plan
100. excerpt — type, proof, format, digest, extract

APPENDIX B

THE SPECIFIC LITERARY SOURCES OF WORDS IN L_1

The Roman numerals correspond to the numerals given for the sources in the experimental arrangement of test words on page 17.

I

1. Like dew on the *gowan* lying
   "Annie Laurie"
8. The Miller was a stout *carl*, for the nones
   Ful big he was of brawn, and eek of bones;
   CHAUCER, *The Prologue*
15. I'm wearin' awa'
    To the land of the *leal*.
    LADY NAIRNE, *The Land of the Leal*
22. The "Little *Gest* of Robin Hood" is a longer composition in which a number of his adventures are woven together into what has sometimes been called a popular epic.
    NEILSON AND THORNDIKE, *A History of English Literature*, p. 65
29. As I was walking all alane
    I heard twa *corbies* making a mane.
    "The Twa Corbies" in ARMES's *Old English Ballads*
36. Flow gently, sweet Afton, among thy green *braes*.
    BURNS, "Afton Water"
43. We twa hae paidlet i' the *burn*
    BURNS, "Auld Lang Syne"
50. Whan word came to the *carline* wife
    That her three sons were gane.
    "The Wife of Usher's Well" in ARMES's *Old English Ballads*
57. For I'm weary wi' hunting, and *fain* wald lie down.
    "Lord Randall" in ARMES's *Old English Ballads*
64. Fare ye weel, my mother dear!
    Fareweel to barn and *byre!*
    "The Wife of Usher's Well" in ARMES's *Old English Ballads*
71. A *cannie* errand to a neibor town.
    BURNS, "The Cotter's Saturday Night"
78. But had I *wist*, before I kist
    That love had been sae ill to win
    "Waly, Waly, Love be Bonny" in ARMES's *Old English Ballads*
85. My sweven (dream) *rede* aright.
    CHAUCER, *The Nonne Preestes Tale*, l. 76
92. A gentle Knight was *pricking* on the plaine.
    SPENSER, *The Faerie Queene*, Book I, l. 1
99. John Anderson, my *jo*, John
    BURNS, "John Anderson My Jo"

Appendix

II

2. The Lesser Children, *A Threnody at the Hunting Season*
   RIDGLEY TORRENCE in RITTENHOUSE'S *The Little Book of Modern Verse*
9. In 1817 the ballad was reprinted in "Sibylline Leaves" with a Latin motto, some textual changes, the marginal *gloss* added . . .
   Notes on *The Rime of the Ancient Mariner*. Academy Classics
16. "Hylas", the celebrated thirteenth idyl of Theocritus is not a *bucolic* poem . . . yet exhibits many touches of the *bucolic* sweetness.
    STEDMAN, *Victorian Poets*, p. 211
23. Say now *Shibboleth;* and he said Sibboleth; for he could not frame to pronounce it right. Judges 12:6
30. Thus Uncle Venner was a miscellaneous old gentleman, partly himself, but, in good measure, somebody else; patched together, too, of different epochs; an *epitome* of times and fashions.
    HAWTHORNE, *The House of the Seven Gables*, Chap. IV. p. 89
37. Our *Apocryphal* Heathen God [Bel] in conjunction with the Dragon.
    ADDISON, *The Spectator* No. 28, par. 6
44. My companion, in a rosier temper, listened with great satisfaction to my *jeremiads*, and ironically concurred.
    STEVENSON, *An Inland Voyage*, p. 18
51. The *dithyramb* was a swinging hymn to Dionysos sung by a chorus of youths sometimes somewhat under the influence of new wine.
    MATTHEWS, *The Developement of the Drama*, II, 42
58. Instead of being chanted in Latin, the plays came to be spoken in the *vernacular*.
    NEILSON and THORNDIKE, *A History of English Literature*, Chap. IV, p. 67
65. And finally in this group there is the fallacy of *analogy*, of attempting proof by a figure of speech.
    BRIGGS and McKINNEY, *Second Book of Composition*, p. 157
72. That it is a distinct *genre* with laws of its own was discovered by Poe in 1842 and discussed by him in what is really the first document in short-story criticism, his review of HAWTHORNE'S *Twice Told Tales*.
    PATTEE, "The Present Stage of the Short Story," *The English Journal*, September, 1923
79. . . . nor if our Fletcher's *aphorism* is true, shall we account this a small influence. "Let me make the songs of a people, and you shall make its laws." CARLYLE, *Essay on Burns*, p. 32
86. He thought it right in a *lexicon* of our language to collect many words which had fallen into disuse.
    BOSWELL, *Life of Johnson*, p. 69
93. But the real Chaucerian school in Scotland begins with "The King's Quair" that is quire, or book, written by James I of Scotland.
    NEILSON AND THORNDIKE, *A History of English Literature*, Chap. III, p. 54
100. (Homer's) constant use of the same *epithets* to his gods and his heroes; such as the "far-darting Phoebus," "the blue-eyed Pallas," "the swift-footed Achilles". POPE, *Translation of Homer*

III

3. That day a feast had been
   Held in high hall, and many a viand left,
   And many a costly *cate*.
   TENNYSON, *Gareth and Lynette*

Appendix B

10. The *sedge* has withered from the lake
    And no birds sing.
    KEATS, "La Belle Dame Sans Merci"
17. O little buds all *bourgeoning* with Spring
    THOMAS S. JONES, JR., "A Song in Spring" in RITTENHOUSE'S *The Little Book of Modern Verse*
24. And *lucent* syrops, tinct with cinnamon.
    KEATS, "The Eve of St. Agnes"
31. . . . found her out to be a serpent, a *lamia*.
    Note on KEATS's *Lamia* quoted in Everyman edition from BURTON's *Anatomy of Melancholy*, Part 3, Sect. 2
38. . . . that accumulated store of gold
    And *orient* gems . . .
    WORDSWORTH, The Excursion, Book IV, 568
45. In vain endeavors to exterminate
    Whom *Obloquy* pursues with hideous bark
    WORDSWORTH, Ecclesiastical Sonnets, II, 14
52. Nought shall make us *rue*,
    If England to itself do rest but true.
    KING JOHN, Act. IV. 2
59. . . . others in Elysian valleys dwell,
    Resting weary limbs at last on beds of *asphodel*.
    TENNYSON, "The Lotos Eaters," l. 170
66. Robed in flames and amber light,
    The clouds in thousand liveries *dight;*
    MILTON, "L'Allegro"
73. At *kith* or kin I needna speir
    Gin I saw ane and twenty.
    BURNS, "And O for Ane and Twenty"
80. . . . so was she sad.
    And heavie sat upon her *palfrey* slow,
    SPENSER, The Faerie Queene, I, 4
87. In vain your *immolated* bulls are slain
    POPE, Iliad XXI, 145
94. Amid the faint companions of their youth,
    With dew all turned to tears; odour, to sighing *ruth*.
    SHELLEY, "Adonais," XVI, 9

IV

4. Our race and blood, a remnant that were left
   Paynim amid their circles, and the stones
   They pitch up straight to heaven:
   TENNYSON, The Holy Grail
5. Two of them were light barks called *caravels* (small light fast ships chiefly Spanish and Portuguese of fifteenth–seventeenth centuries)
   IRVING, Columbus
11. He will have a heavy miss of such a *paladin* as you are, if the truce should break off.
    SCOTT, Quentin Durward, p. 38
12. Press where ye see my white plume shine amidst the ranks of war,
    And be your *oriflamme* today the helmet of Navarre.
    MACAULAY, "Battle of Ivry"

Appendix

18. Cracked *basilisks* and splinter'd cockatrices
    And shatter'd talbots, which had left the stones
    Raw that they fell from.
    TENNYSON, *The Holy Grail*

19. Nay, were there not in that clear logically founded Transcendentalism of thine; still more, in meek, silent, deep-seated *Sans-culottism* . . . the visible rudiments of such speculation?
    CARLYLE, *Sartor Resartus*, Chap. III, p. 13
    . . . the epithet *Sansculotte* first gets applied to indigent Patriotism. (Note on above.)

25. No *jongleur* can show so deft a transmutation.
    SCOTT, *The Talisman*

26. . . . and did sacrifice to Apollo, even unblemished *hecatombs* of bulls and goats, along the shore of the unvintaged sea; and the sweet savor arose to heaven eddying amid the smoke.
    HOMER, *The Iliad*, p. 11

32. Never herald went from the court of Burgundy without having cause to cry '*Largess*'.
    SCOTT, *Quentin Durward*, p. 501

33. Thou wretched Outcast, from the gift of fire
    And food cut off by *sacerdotal* ire,
    From every sympathy that Man bestowed!
    WORDSWORTH, *Ecclesiastical Sonnets*. Series I, Druidical Excommunication

39. *Gammer Gurton's Needle*
    WILLIAM STEVENSON

40. O for some drowsy Morphean *amulet!*
    KEATS, "The Eve of St. Agnes"

46. And while the young lambs bound
    As to the *tabor's* sound.
    WORDSWORTH, "Ode on the Intimations of Immortality"

47. . . . a broad and shadowy hat, with cockle shells stitched on its brim, and a long staff shod with iron, to the upper end of which was attached a branch of palm, completed the *Palmer's* attire.
    SCOTT, *Ivanhoe*, Chap. III, p. 42

53. In 1806, Irving returned home; the next year in company with William Irving and James Kirke Paulding, he began writing a series of essays called "*Salmagundi*".
    (Footnote: applied to literature it means a collection of miscellaneous essays.)
    WENDELL and GREENOUGH, *History of Literature in America*

54. Save one old *beldam*, weak in body and in soul.
    KEATS, "The Eve of St. Agnes"

60. It is a monument of Gothic insecurity, all turreted, and *gargoyled*, and slashed, and bedizened with half a score of architectural fancies.
    Stevenson, *An Inland Voyage*, p. 155

61. To be insulted, *flagellated*, and even executed as a malefactor.
    SMOLLETT, *Humphrey Clinker*, II, 173

67. Tanned face of June, the *nomad* gipsy, laughs
    Above her widespread wares.
    FRANCIS LEDWIDGE; "June," in WILKINSON'S *Contemporary Verse*

68. The *Hospice* of St. Bernard.

Appendix B

74. He in celestial *panoply* all arm'd
    Of radiant Urim, work divinely wrought,
    Ascended.
    MILTON, *Paradise Lost*, VI, 760

75. There, where your *argosies* with portly sail,
    Like signiors and rich burghers of the flood,
    Or, as it were, the pageants of the sea.
    The Merchant of Venice, I, 1, 9

81. . . . the . . . (ill endowed by nature) on the other hand is our *Philistine*.
    (Arnold's name for the middle class of English Society, whose defect he declares to be narrowness).
    ARNOLD, *Culture and Anarchy*, Chap. I in Newcomer and Andrews

82. . . . they might turn down yonder wild glade, which would bring them to the hermitage of Copmanhurst, where a pious *anchoret* would make them sharers for the night of the shelter of his roof and the benefit of his prayers.
    SCOTT, *Ivanhoe*, p. 11

88. A long street climbs to one tall-tower'd mill;
    And high in heaven behind it a gray down
    With Danish *barrows*.
    TENNYSON, *Enoch Arden*

89. . . . and it is out of the Latin *liturgy* of the Christian Church that the drama of the modern European languages has been slowly developed.
    BRANDER MATTHEWS, *The Development of the Drama*

95. He (Wamba) bore like his companion, a *scrip* attached to his belt.
    SCOTT, *Ivanhoe*, Chap. I

V

6. (Carlyle) is the most shining *avatar* of whim the world has ever seen.
   LOWELL, *My Study Windows*, p. 148

13. No Skald in song has told
    No *Saga* taught thee!
    LONGFELLOW, "The Skeleton in Armor"

20. for the *bruit* goeth shrewdly out, . . .
    SCOTT, *Ivanhoe*, Chap. XXX, 384

27. At the Christmas season in English country places you may still see the village actors or *mummers* perform a play in which some one is killed and then brought to life by the doctor.
    NEILSON AND THORNDIKE, *History of English Literature*

34. Where was thine *aegis*, Pallas, that appalled stern Alaric.
    BYRON, *Childe Harold*, II, 14

41. At what precise minute that little airy musician doffs his nightgear, and prepares to tune up his unseasonable *matins*, we are not naturalists enough to determine.
    LAMB, *Essays of Elia*, "That We Should Rise with the Lark"

48. If any man loveth not the Lord, let him be *anathema*.
    I Corinthians 16:22

55. Wild *Bacchanal* of truth's mysterious wine,
    SHELLEY, "Ode to Liberty," XIV, 5

62. To what a *fortuitous* concurrence do we not owe every pleasure and convenience of our lives?
    GOLDSMITH, *Vicar of Wakefield*, Chap. XXXI

69. The dim floor work in front is *antiphonal* to the wealth of water beyond.
    SWINBURNE, *Essays and Studies*, p. 373

48 Appendix

76. There were *cabals* breaking out in the company
   IRVING, *Tales of a Traveler*, II, 30

83. Most words, from their use acquire special *connotations* or associations which almost seem to give them a character of their own.
   GREENOUGH AND KITTREDGE, *Words and Their Ways in English Speech*, Chap. XVI, p. 224

90. By his Skill in *Necromancy* he had a power of calling whom he pleaseth from the Dead.
   SWIFT, *Gulliver's Travels*, III, VII

97. Great is thy name in the *rubric*, thou venerable arch-flamen of Hymen!
   LAMB, *Essays of Elia*, "Valentine's Day"

VI

7. . . . who would these *fardels* bear
   To grunt and sweat under a weary life.
   Hamlet, III, 1, 76

14. My lord, he's going to his mother's closet
    Behind the *arras* I'll convey myself.
    Hamlet, III, 3, 28

21. The fair Ophelia! Nymph, in thy *orisons*
    Be all my sins remember'd.
    Hamlet, III, 1, 89

28. Ay, *springes* to catch woodcocks.
    Hamlet, I, 3, 15

35. Who, dipping all his faults in their affection
    Would, like the spring that turneth wood to stone,
    Convert his *gyves* to graces:
    Hamlet, I, 5, 24

42. Ne'er a villain dwelling in all Denmark
    But he's an *arrant* knave.
    Hamlet, I, 5, 24

49. . . . for who shall go about
    To *cozen* fortune and be honorable
    Without the stamp of merit?
    Merchant of Venice, II, 9, 38

56. Here lives a *caitiff* wretch would sell it him.
    Romeo and Juliet, V, 1, 52

63. The undiscover'd country from whose *bourn*
    No traveller returns.
    Hamlet, III, 1, 79

70. This my hand will rather
    The multitudinous seas *incarnadine*
    Making the green one red.
    Macbeth, II, 2, 62

77. . . . I might not this believe
    Without the sensible and true *avouch*
    Of mine own eyes.
    Hamlet, I, 1, 57

84. That runs lolling up and down to hide his *bauble* in a hole.
    Romeo and Juliet, II, 4, 97

98. . . . to whose falls
    Melodious birds sing *madrigals*.
    Merry Wives of Windsor, III, 1, 18

The sources of the quotations listed for L_1 are here arranged by author and title. The figures after the specific titles refer to the following:

1. Listed in College Entrance Requirements.[1]

[1] Hudelson, E. "Our Courses of Study in Literature." *The English Journal*, September, 1923.

Appendix B   49

2. Duplicated in Secondary School and College Curricula.[2]
3. Listed in Secondary School Courses of Study,[3]
4. Listed in Index to Books for Home Reading for High School and Junior High School prepared for The National Council of Teachers of English.

ADDISON, *The Spectator* 4
ARMES, *Old English Ballads* 1, 4
ARNOLD, *Culture and Anarchy* (Newcomer and Andrews) 3, 4
Bible
BOSWELL, *Life of Johnson* 1, 4
BRIGGS AND MCKINNEY, *Second Book of Composition*
BURNS, "Afton Water" 1
    "And O for Ane and Twenty" 1
    "Auld Lang Syne" 1
    "John Anderson My Jo" 1
    "The Cotter's Saturday Night" 1, 2, 4
BYRON, *Childe Harold* 2, 4
CARLYLE, *Essay on Burns* 1, 4
    Sartor Resartus 4
CHAUCER, *The Prologue* 1, 4
    The Nonne Preestes Tale
COLERIDGE, *The Rime of the Ancient Mariner* 1, 2
GOLDSMITH, *The Vicar of Wakefield* 1, 4
GREENOUGH and KITTREDGE, *Words and Their Ways in English Speech*
HAWTHORNE, *The House of the Seven Gables* 1, 4
HOMER, *The Iliad* (Leaf and Lang tr.), 1, 4
IRVING, *Columbus*
    Tales of a Traveler 3, 4
JONES, T. S., Jr. "A Song of Spring"
KEATS, "La Belle Dame Sans Merci" 1
    "Lamia" 1
    "The Eve of St. Agnes" 1
LAMB, *Essays of Elia* 1, 4
LEDWIDGE, "June"
LONGFELLOW, "The Skeleton in Armor" 3
LOWELL, *My Study Windows* 4
MACAULAY, "Battle of Ivry"
MATTHEWS, *The Development of the Drama*
MILTON, "L'Allegro" 1, 2, 4
    Paradise Lost 4
NAIRNE, "The Land of the Leal" 3
NEILSON and THORNDIKE, *A History of English Literature*
PATTEE, "Present Stage of Short Story." *The English Journal*, September, 1923
POPE, *The Iliad* 3
    Translation of Homer
SCOTT, *Ivanhoe* 1, 2, 4
    Quentin Durward 1, 4
    The Talisman
SHAKESPEARE, *Hamlet* 1, 2, 4
    King John
    Macbeth 1, 2, 4

[2] Noble, S. G. "The Duplication of Elementary and Secondary Subject-Matter in College English," Table I, *The English Journal*, January, 1923.
[3] Hudelson, E. "Our Courses of Study in Literature." *The English Journal*, September, 1923.

                Merchant of Venice 1, 2, 4
                Merry Wives of Windsor
                Romeo and Juliet 1
SHELLEY, "Adonais" 1, 4
                "Ode to Liberty"
SMOLLETT, Humphrey Clinker
SPENSER, The Fairie Queene 3, 4
STEDMAN, Victorian Poets
STEVENSON, R. L. An Inland Voyage
STEVENSON, W. Gammer Gurton's Needle
SWIFT, Gulliver's Travels
SWINBURNE, Essays and Studies
TENNYSON, Enoch Arden 1, 2, 4
                Gareth and Lynette 1, 2, 4
                The Holy Grail 1, 2, 4
                "The Lotos Eaters" 1
TORRENCE, "The Lesser Children" (in New Voices) 3, 4
WENDELL and GREENOUGH, History of Literature in America
WORDSWORTH, Ecclesiastical Sonnets
                The Excursion
                "Ode on Intimations of Immortality" 1

THE SPECIFIC LITERARY SOURCES OF WORDS IN L_2

I

1. And when the king of the city, which was *cleped* Estorause, saw the fellowship . . .
    MALORY, *Le Morte Darthur*, Book XVII, Chap. 19. (Newcomer and Andrews)
8. The nut-brown bride has oxen, brother,
    The nut-brown bride has *kye;*
        "Lord Thomas and Fair Annet" in ARMES's *Old English Ballads*
15. *Warlocks* and witches in a dance
                                BURNS, "Tam O'Shanter"
22. "*Hind* Horn fair, and Hind Horn free,
    O where were you born, in what countrie?"
                "Hind Horn" in ARMES's *Old English Ballads*
29. Man, art thou *fey!*
                                SCOTT, *Fair Maid of Perth*
36. (So priketh hem nature in hir *corages*):
    Than longen folk to goon on pilgrimages,
                                CHAUCER, *The Prologue*
43. That every *wight* to shrowd it did constrain,
    And this faire couple eke to shroud themselves were fain.
            SPENSER, *The Faerie Queene*, Book I, Canto 1, Stanza 6
50. *Irks* care the crop-full bird?
                                BROWNING, "Rabbi Ben Ezra"
57. Curled *minion*, dancer, coiner of sweet words!
                                ARNOLD, "Sohrab and Rustum"
64. O Johnnie, for my *benison*
    I beg you'll stay at home.
            "Johnnie Cock" in ARMES's *Old English Ballads*

Appendix B

71. O'er moor and *fen*, o'er crag and torrent, till
     The night is gone
     NEWMAN, "Lead, Kindly Light"
78. "I fear," said the Black Knight, "I fear greatly, that there is no one here that is qualified to take upon him, for the *nonce*, this same character of father confessor."
     SCOTT, *Ivanhoe*, Chap. XXV
85. Despair, and *fell* disease and ghastly Poverty
     GRAY, "Hymn to Adversity" (*Golden Treasury*)
92. In somer, when the *shawes* be sheyne,
     "Robin Hood and The Monk." (Newcomer and Andrews)
99. Hope of new good *hap* he gan to feel.
     SPENSER, *The Faerie Queen*, Book I, Canto 3, Stanza 34

II

2. This is worth several *homilies* on Mercy; for it is the voice of Mercy herself.
    CARLYLE, *Essay on Burns*, Paragraph 24
9. (The Shepherd's Calendar) consists of twelve pastoral poems, or *eclogues*, one for each month of the year.
    LONG, *English Literature*
16. Thieves' slang or peddlers' French (*argot*, Rothwalsch) . . . is, in fact, the professional jargon of a particular class of society, and is comparable, therefore, to other technical vocabularies.
    GREENOUGH and KITTREDGE, *Words and Their Ways*. Chap. IV, p. 55
23. Grolier was one of the earliest of the great *bibliophiles* of France.
    BRANDER MATTHEWS
30. The simplest form of *apologue* is the fable.
    HEYDRICK, *Types of the Short Story*
37. . . . yet ordinarily, whether we are too clumsy for so subtle a topic, or from whatever cause, as soon as men begin to write on nature, they fall into *euphuism*.
    EMERSON, "Nature"
44. "*Elegy* Written in a Country Churchyard"
    GRAY
51. Clasped like a *missal* where swart Paynims pray
    KEATS, "The Eve of St. Agnes"
58. *Vignettes in Rhyme*
    DOBSON
65. To this last *apothegm* poor Hepzibah responded with a sigh . . .
    HAWTHORNE, *The House of the Seven Gables*, Chap. IV, p. 94
72. The ode is usually composed of lines of varying length, and divided into stanzas, or *strophes*.
    Newcomer's "The Study of Poetry" in PALGRAVE, *The Golden Treasury* (Lake)
79. No novelist has written dialogue more sparkling with *epigram*, or put into the mouths of his (Meredith's) characters more concentrated wisdom.
    NEILSON and THORNDIKE, *A History of English Literature*, Chap. XVI
86. He again hints: 'At a time when the divine Commandment, Thou shalt not steal, wherein truly, if well understood, is comprised the whole

Decalogue, with Solon's and Lycurgus's Constitutions, Justinian's *Pandects* . . .
CARLYLE, *Sartor Resartus*, Chap. X, p. 181

93. May bards from crickets learn their *canticles!*
MACKAYE, "Uriel" in RITTENHOUSE'S *The Little Book of Modern Verse*

100. Papers from the 'Quarterly Review' together with certain *excerpts* from the 'Register'
SOUTHEY, *Letters*

III

3. Bring the *rathe* primrose that forsaken dies.
MILTON, "Lycidas"

10. . . . Gareth, in a showerful spring
Stared at the *spate*.
TENNYSON, *Gareth and Lynette*

17. Round the elm-tree *bole* are in tiny leaf.
BROWNING, "Home Thoughts from Abroad"

24. In a *coign* of the cliff between lowland and highland
SWINBURNE, "A Forsaken Garden"

31. The youth of green *savannahs* spake

38. What pipes and *timbrels?* What wild ecstasy?
WORDSWORTH, "Ruth"
KEATS, "Ode on a Grecian Urn"

45. My good blade carves the *casques* of men
TENNYSON, *Sir Galahad*

52. His wee bit *ingle* blinkin' bonnilie
BURNS, "The Cotter's Saturday Night"

59. Where perhaps some beauty lies
The *cynosure* of neighboring eyes.

66. At length burst in the *argent* revelry
MILTON, "L'Allegro"
KEATS, "The Eve of St. Agnes"

73. The seat of desolation, void of light
Save what the glimmering of these *livid* flames
Casts pale and dreadful?

80. "A *boon*, Sir King—this quest!"
MILTON, *Paradise Lost*, Book I
TENNYSON, *Gareth and Lynette*, l. 632

87. Without the *meed* of some melodious tear

94. And when they list, their lean and flashy songs
Grate on their *scrannel pipes* of wretched straw;
MILTON, "Lycidas"
MILTON, "Lycidas"

4. Go home with thy ships and company and lord it among thy *Myrmidons.*
HOMER, *Iliad*, (Leaf and Lang tr.), Book I

IV

5. When *chapman* billies leave the street

11. "Nirvana"
BURNS, "Tam O'Shanter"
JOHN HALL WHEELOCK in Wilkinson's *New Voices*

12. In place of these, he was equipped with a sword of lath, resembling that with which *Harlequin* operates his wonders upon the modern stage.
SCOTT, *Ivanhoe*, Chap. I

Appendix B

18. . . . for they make broad their *phylacteries*, and enlarge the borders of their garments.
MATTHEW 23:5
19. When maidens sing sweet *barcarolles*
MOORE, "Venetian Air"
25. Voice of the *Leprechaun* singing shrill
As he merrily plies his trade
YEATS, *Fairy and Folk Tales*
26. The new *apocalypse* of nature.
CARLYLE, *Sartor Resartus*, II, V
32. There has lately been found a Humane Tooth in a *catacomb* (at Rome)
STEELE, *The Tatler*, No. 129
33. The herald . . . was dressed in a *tabard*, or coat, embroidered with the arms of his master.
SCOTT, *Quentin Durward*, Chap. XXXIII, p. 497
39. A house that changes its inhabitants so often, and receives such a perpetual succession of guests, is not a Palace, but a *caravansary*.
ADDISON, *The Spectator*, No. 289
40. O sing praises unto the Lord. Selah.
Psalm 68
46. As we the *Berserk's* tale
Measured in cups of ale
LONGFELLOW, "The Skeleton in Armor"
47. Many a *wassail* bout
Wore the long Winter out;
LONGFELLOW, "The Skeleton in Armor"
53. The lazy engines of outlandish birth,
Couched like a king each on its bank of earth—
Arbalist, manganel and catapult
BROWNING, *Sordello*, IV, 362
54. Out of my stony griefs
Bethels I'll raise
ADAMS, SARAH FLOWER, "Nearer, My God, to Thee"
60. In Sagittarius, however, Teufelsdrockh begins to shew himself even more than usually *sibylline*.
CARLYLE, *Sartor Resartus*, Chap. III, p. 98, Sibylline Books
61. It was now *kermis* or a fair in this town.
EVELYN, *Diary*, 28 July
67. The whole East dates its era from this Flight, *Hegira*, as they name it: the year 1 of this *Hegira* is 622 of our Era, the fifty-third of Mahomet's life.
CARLYLE, "The Hero as Prophet"
68. . . . like *genii* enfranchised from their glass phial.
CARLYLE, *Sartor Resartus*, Chap. VI, p. 135
74. Vogelweid the *Minnesinger*,
When he left this world of ours
LONGFELLOW, "Walter von der Vogelweid'
75. It is he that saith not '*Kismet*'; it is he that knows not Fate;
CHESTERTON, "Lepanto" in WILKINSON'S *New Voices*
81. The weird *palimpsest* old and vast,
Wherein thou hid'st the spectral past.
WHITTIER, "Snowbound"

54 Appendix

82. . . . by the close of that century (the seventeenth) fiction was flourishing in various forms, long romances of love and honor, *picaresque* stories of rogues and their rascalities. . .
   NEILSON and THORNDIKE, *A History of English Literature*, Chap. XI
88. Bows were bent and *harquebusses* were aimed at him from the walls.
   SCOTT, *Quentin Durward*, Chap. VII, p. 111
89. The voice of the *seneschal* flared like a torch
   LOWELL, *The Vision of Sir Launfal*
94. Stately Spanish *galleon* coming from the Isthmus
   MASEFIELD, "Cargoes"
95. *Quinquereme* of Nineveh from distant Ophir
   MASEFIELD, "Cargoes"

V

6. . . . a danger . . . lest . . . we should unwarily conclude friendship a false ideal good, a mere *utopian* pleasure.
   COWPER
13. While, like a *tutelary* Power,
   He stands there fixed from hour to hour.
   WORDSWORTH, *The White Doe of Rylstone* III, 175
20. Burke's observations on the *apotheosis* were admirable.
   MACAULAY, *Essay on Hastings*
27. Sweet-shaped lightnings from the *nadir* deep.
   KEATS, *Hyperion*, l. 276
34. Paris, teeming beneath a very courtly exterior, with *mordant* words
   PATER
41. Two horses have emerged from the *ruck* and are sweeping, rushing, storming towards us, almost side by side.
   HOLMES, *Our Hundred Days*
48. Mirth and opium, ratafia and tears
   The daily *anodyne*, and nightly draught
   To kill those foes to fair ones, time and thought.
   POPE, *Moral Essays*, II
55. Or what (though rare) of later age
   Ennobled hath the *buskined* stage.
   MILTON, *Il Penseroso*
62. Though in the *apogee*
   Of time there sit no individual
   Godhead of life.
   MACKAYE, P., "Uriel" in RITTENHOUSE'S *The Little Book of Modern Verse*
69. That's but a *cavil;* he is old, I young.
   Taming of the Shrew, II, l. 392
76. Pythagoras elucidated the *arcana* of nature.
   IRVING, *Knickerbocker History of New York*, p. 43
83. There is another very efficacious method for subduing the most obstinate, *contumacious* sinner.
   HAMMOND
90. For great men I have ever had the warmest *predilection*.
   CARLYLE
97. Surrounded by this *arabesque* work of his musing fancy.
   DICKENS, *Dombey and Son*, p. 105

Appendix B

VI

7. A *murrain* on your monster!
   The Tempest, III, 2, 88
14. For fear thy very stones *prate* of my whereabout
    Macbeth, II, 1, 58
21. This *grisly* beast, which Lion hight by name
    A Midsummer Night's Dream, V, 1, 138
28. *Avaunt!* and quit my sight! let the earth hide thee!
    Macbeth, III, 4, 93
35. He lends out money gratis and brings down
    The rate of *usance* here with us in Venice.
    The Merchant of Venice, I, 3, 42
42. I have drugged their *possets*
    That death and nature do contend.
    Macbeth, II, 2, 6
49. We are men, my *liege*.
    Macbeth, III, 1, 91
56. *Sooth*, madam, I hear nothing.
    Julius Caesar, II, 4, 20
63. Will his vouchers vouch him no more of his purchases, and double ones, too, than the length and breadth of a pair of *indentures?*
    Hamlet, V, 1, 102
70. Thriftless ambition, that wilt *ravin* up
    Thine own life's means.
    Macbeth, II, 4, 28
77. When he himself might his *quietus* make
    With a bare bodkin?
    Hamlet, III, 1, 75
84. And be these juggling fiends no more believed
    That *palter* with us in a double sense.
    Macbeth, I, 8, 20
91. Most brisky juvenal, and *eke* most lovely Jew.
    A Midsummer Night's Dream, III, 1, 85
98. I'll *amerce* you with so strong a fine
    That you shall all repent the loss of mine.
    Romeo and Juliet, III, 1, 195

The sources of the quotations listed for L_2 are arranged and marked in the same fashion indicated for L_1.

ADAMS, "Nearer, My God, to Thee"
ADDISON, *The Spectator* 4
ARMES, *Old English Ballads* 1, 4
ARNOLD, *Sohrab and Rustum* 1, 4
Bible
BROWNING, "Home Thoughts from Abroad" 1, 4
   "Rabbi Ben Ezra" 1, 4
   "Sordello"
BURNS, "Tam O'Shanter" 1, 4
   "The Cotter's Saturday Night" 1, 2, 4
CARLYLE, *Essay on Burns* 1
   Heroes and Hero Worship 3
   Sartor Resartus 4
CHAUCER, *The Prologue* 1, 4
CHESTERTON, "Lepanto" (in *New Voices*) 4
DICKENS, *Dombey and Son* 4
DOBSON, *Vignettes in Rhyme*
EMERSON, *Nature* 1, 4

Appendix

EVELYN, *Diary*
GRAY, "Elegy Written in a Country Churchyard" 1
    "Hymn to Adversity"
GREENOUGH and KITTREDGE, *Words and Their Ways in English Speech*
HAWTHORNE, *The House of the Seven Gables* 1, 4
HEYDRICK, *Types of Short Story* 1, 4
HOLMES, *Our Hundred Days*
HOMER, *The Iliad* (Leaf and Lang tr.)
IRVING, *Knickerbocker History of New York*
KEATS, "Hyperion"
    "Ode on a Grecian Urn" 1, 4
    "The Eve of St. Agnes" 1, 4
LONG, *English Literature*
LONGFELLOW, "The Skeleton in Armor" 3, 4
    "Walter von der Vogelweid 3, 4
LOWELL, "The Vision of Sir Launfal" 1, 2, 4
MALORY, *Le Morte Darthur* (Newcomer and Andrews) 1, 4
MACAULAY, *Essay on Hastings* 4
MACKAYE, "Uriel" (Rittenhouse) 4
MASEFIELD, "Cargoes" 4
MILTON, "Il Penseroso" 1, 2, 4
    "L'Allegro" 1, 2, 4
    "Lycidas" 1, 2, 4
    Paradise Lost, Book I
MOORE, "Venetian Air"
NEILSON and THORNDIKE, *A History of English Literature*
NEWCOMER and ANDREWS, *Twelve Centuries of English Prose and Poetry*
NEWMAN, "Lead Kindly Light"
PALGRAVE, *The Golden Treasury* 1, 4
PATER, *Essays*
POPE, *Moral Essays*
SCOTT, *Fair Maid of Perth*
    Ivanhoe 1, 2, 4
    Quentin Durward 1, 4
SHAKESPEARE, *A Midsummer Night's Dream* 1, 4
    Hamlet 1, 2, 4
    Julius Caesar 1, 2, 4
    Macbeth 1, 2, 4
    Merchant of Venice 1, 2, 4
    Romeo and Juliet 1
    The Taming of the Shrew
    The Tempest 1
SOUTHEY, *Letters*
SPENSER, *The Faerie Queene* 3, 4
STEELE, *The Tatler* 4
SWINBURNE, "A Forsaken Garden" 4
TENNYSON, *Gareth and Lynette* 1, 2, 4
    Sir Galahad
WHEELOCK, "Nirvana" (*New Voices*) 4
WHITTIER, "Snowbound" 1, 4
WORDSWORTH, "Ruth"
    "The White Doe of Rylstone."
YEATS, *Fairy and Folk Tales* 4

APPENDIX C

ALPHABETICAL LIST OF WORDS IN L₁ AND L₂ SHOWING THE ORDER OF DIFFICULTY OF THE TEST WORDS AS FOUND BY EXPERIMENT

L_1	Number [1] in L_1	Rank [2] by English Teachers	Rank [2] by Others	Permille [3] Correct by English Teachers	Permille [3] Correct by Others
1. aegis	34	35	20	411	429
2. amulet	40	78	78	696	837
3. analogy	65	96	97	898	959
4. anathema	48	83	74	735	776
5. anchorite	82	77	71	691	755
6. antiphonal	69	60	56	543	673
7. aphorism	79	70	52	637	653
8. apocryphal	37	39	46	433	612
9. argosy	75	51	32	506	510
10. arrant ..... (7)*	42	8	16	180	388
11. arras	14	91	43	825	592
12. asphodel	59	68	72	620	776
13. avatar	6	6	9	153	286
14. avouch	77	64	19	582	408
15. bacchanal	55	97	93	900	939
16. barrow ..... (4)*	88	24	25	328	469
17. basilisk	18	13	23	248	449
18. bauble .... (5)*	84	82	89	730	898
19. beldam	54	62	48	552	633
20. bourn	63	31	21	394	429
21. brae	36	67	64	608	714
22. bruit	20	38	36	418	531
23. bucolic	16	57	62	533	714
24. burgeon	17	18	14	299	388
25. burn .... (1 a 5)*	43	36	38	414	531
26. byre	64	5	11	148	327
27. cabal	76	55	70	523	755
28. caitiff	56	17	27	285	490
29. canny	71	80	94	703	939
30. caravel	5	19	42	304	592
31. carl	8	52	58	509	694
32. carline	50	3	1	129	122
33. cates	3	28	17	380	408
34. connotation	83	63	74	577	776
35. corbie	29	26	26	353	490

[1] This means the position of the word in the test as given.
[2] This means the rank of the word as found by experiment. (1=hard, 100=easy.)
[3] This means the permille correct of the 406 English teachers and the 49 other persons who took both forms of the tests (L₁ and L₂.)
* Credit number as given in Thorndike's *The Teacher's Word Book*.

Appendix

ALPHABETICAL LIST OF WORDS IN L₁ AND L₂ SHOWING THE ORDER OF DIFFICULTY OF THE TEST WORDS AS FOUND BY EXPERIMENT—*(Continued)*

L_1	Number[1] in L_1	Rank[2] by English Teachers	Rank[2] by Others	Permille[3] Correct by English Teachers	Permille[3] Correct by Others
36. cozen	49	33	44	409	592
37. dight	66	76	50	669	653
38. dithyramb	51	15	6	273	245
39. epithet	100	56	75	530	776
40. epitome	30	88	84	808	898
41. fain ...... (8)*......	57	90	100	825	1,000
42. fardel	7	32	22	394	449
43. flagellate	61	50	73	504	776
44. fortuitous	62	37	79	418	837
45. gammer	39	53	47	518	633
46. gargoyle	60	86	86	769	898
47. genre	72	71	94	637	939
48. gest...............	22	29	15	389	388
49. gloss ...... (5)*.....	9	22	18	319	408
50. gowan	1	9	8	180	265
51. gyve	35	42	37	457	531
52. hecatomb	26	34	40	409	551
53. hospice	68	69	80	633	837
54. immolate	87	25	29	336	490
55. incarnadine	70	65	49	591	633
56. jeremiad	44	48	67	472	735
57. jo	99	46	60	465	694
58. jongleur	25	49	31	472	510
59. kith	73	4	2	141	122
60. lamia	31	2	12	124	347
61. largesse	32	59	55	540	673
62. leal	15	27	53	365	673
63. lexicon	86	89	83	822	878
64. liturgy	89	85	91	762	918
65. lucent	24	94	92	856	939
66. madrigal	98	44	57	462	673
67. matins ..... (4)*....	41	99	95	944	959
68. mummer	27	41	54	445	673
69. necromancy	90	79	65	698	714
70. nomad ..... (4)*....	67	100	98	966	980

[1] This means the position of the word in the test as given.
[2] This means the rank of the word as found by experiment. (1=hard, 100=easy.)
[3] This means the permille correct of the 406 English teachers and the 49 other persons who took both forms of the tests (L_1 and L_2).
*Credit number as given in Thorndike's *The Teacher's Word Book*.

Appendix C

ALPHABETICAL LIST OF WORDS IN L₁ AND L₂ SHOWING THE ORDER OF DIFFICULTY OF THE TEST WORDS AS FOUND BY EXPERIMENT—(*Continued*)

L₁	Number[1] in L₁	Rank[2] by English Teachers	Rank[2] by Others	Permille[3] Correct by English Teachers	Permille[3] Correct by Others
71. obloquy	45	20	24	309	469
72. orient ...(13 5 a)*...	38	7	3	165	163
73. oriflamme	12	10	35	190	531
74. orison	21	84	66	745	735
75. paladin	11	61	61	545	714
76. palfrey .....(4)*	80	74	69	657	735
77. palmer	47	92	59	827	694
78. panoply	74	30	28	394	490
79. paynim	4	23	34	326	531
80. philistine ..(10 5 b)*..	81	75	88	669	898
81. pricking ..(19 3 b)*..	92	16	13	285	367
82. quair	93	12	7	248	245
83. rede	85	21	33	314	510
84. rubric	97	1	10	100	286
85. rue ....(8)*	52	93	96	856	959
86. ruth	94	58	77	540	816
87. sacerdotal	33	72	63	640	714
88. saga	13	95	82	869	878
89. salmagundi	53	54	68	521	735
90. sansculotte	19	11	30	219	510
91. savant	96	87	99	791	980
92. scrip	95	45	41	462	551
93. sedge	10	66	76	606	796
94. shibboleth	23	73	81	650	857
95. springes	28	43	45	460	612
96. tabor ......(7)*	46	40	39	443	531
97. thorp	91	14	4	270	184
98. threnody	2	47	12	465	347
99. vernacular	58	98	57	903	673
100. wist ......(4)*	78	81	88	723	898

[1] This means the position of the word in the test as given.
[2] This means the rank of the word as found by experiment. (1=hard, 100=easy.)
[3] This means the permille correct of the 406 English teachers and the 49 other persons who took both forms of the tests (L₁ and L₂).
*Credit number as given in Thorndike's *The Teacher's Word Book*.

Alphabetical List of Words in L_1 and L_2 Showing the Order of Difficulty of the Test Words as Found by Experiment—(Continued)

L_2	Number in L_2	Rank by English Teachers	Rank by Others	Permille Correct by English Teachers	Permille Correct by Others
1. amerce	98	3	9	058	265
2. anodyne	48	75	78	659	796
3. apologue	30	31	19	375	408
4. apocalypse	26	97	89	898	878
5. apogee	62	61	67	552	714
6. apothegm	65	68	65	579	694
7. apotheosis	20	28	56	360	653
8. arabesque	97	52	17	504	388
9. arbalest	53	18	40	258	571
10. arcana	76	9	27	197	490
11. argent	66	88	92	803	898
12. argot	16	46	48	474	612
13. avaunt	28	86	86	774	857
14. barcarole	19	79	77	715	796
15. benison	64	92	91	871	878
16. berserk	46	34	54	392	633
17. bethel	54	56	49	523	612
18. bibliophile	23	40	66	423	714
19. bole	17	19	22	263	469
20. boon ...(11 5 b)*...	80	94	84	883	837
21. buskin	55	16	8	243	245
22. canticle	93	70	60	596	653
23. caravansary	39	35	53	397	633
24. casque .....(5)*.....	45	80	83	725	837
25. catacomb	32	99	96	920	959
26. cavil	69	42	68	433	714
27. chapman	5	49	45	491	592
28. cleped	1	37	82	409	837
29. coign	24	41	26	431	490
30. contumacious	83	2	1	071	082
31. corages	36	24	20	333	408
32. cynosure	59	93	72	871	755
33. eclogue	9	73	33	652	551
34. eke ......(4)*......	91	47	47	477	592
35. elegy	44	85	62	754	673
36. epigram	79	87	98	798	980
37. euphuism	37	78	38	710	571
38. excerpt	100	90	95	854	939
39. fell ....(67 1 b)*...	85	60	32	543	531
40. fen ....(6)*......	71	62	76	557	776
41. fey	29	1	3	058	163
42. galleon	95	90	85	854	837
43. genie	68	84	87	752	857
44. grisly	21	7	18	163	408
45. hap ....(7)......	99	65	63	567	673

Appendix C 61

ALPHABETICAL LIST OF WORDS IN L_1 AND L_2 SHOWING THE ORDER OF DIFFICULTY OF THE TEST WORDS AS FOUND BY EXPERIMENT—(*Continued*)

L_2	Number in L_2	Rank by English Teachers	Rank by Others	Permille Correct by English Teachers	Permille Correct by Others
46. harlequin	12	81	75	727	776
47. harquebus	88	5	11	151	306
48. hegira	67	61	59	552	653
49. hind ....(23 3 a)*...	22	54	34	513	551
50. homily	2	50	61	496	673
51. indenture	63	59	73	540	755
52. ingle	52	25	14	343	347
53. irk	50	82	93	730	918
54. kermis	61	13	5	214	224
55. kismet	75	48	69	482	735
56. kye	8	63	21	562	429
57. leprechaun	25	30	37	367	571
58. liege ......(7)*.....	49	98	94	905	939
59. livid	73	11	15	204	367
60. meed ......(5)*.....	87	76	81	691	816
61. minion .....(5)*.....	57	66	64	569	694
62. minnesinger	74	51	41	496	571
63. missal	51	58	57	540	653
64. mordant	34	12	29	207	531
65. murrain	7	53	51	506	633
66. myrmidon	4	20	44	273	592
67. nadir	27	26	46	350	592
68. nirvana	11	38	52	411	633
69. nonce	78	64	80	564	816
70. palimpsest	81	21	31	304	531
71. palter	84	27	25	350	469
72. pandect	86	15	42	241	571
73. phylactery	18	14	23	241	469
74. picaroon	82	37	12	409	327
75. posset	42	55	39	513	571
76. prate ......(7)*.....	14	100	100	946	1,000
77. predilection	90	45	74	453	755
78. quietus	77	39	50	416	612
79. quinquereme	96	43	55	450	633
80. rathe	3	50	2	496	143
81. ravin	70	22	10	307	306
82. ruck	41	20	4	273	224
83. savannah	31	32	35	387	551
84. scrannel pipes	94	36	28	406	510
85. selah	40	8	7	178	245
86. seneschal	89	69	43	589	571
87. shawes	92	6	13	158	327
88. sibylline	60	74	58	655	653
89. sooth ......(8)*.....	56	91	90	856	878
90. spate	10	33	6	392	245

Appendix

ALPHABETICAL LIST OF WORDS IN L_1 AND L_2 SHOWING THE ORDER OF DIFFICULTY OF THE TEST WORDS AS FOUND BY EXPERIMENT—(*Concluded*)

L_2	Number in L_2	Rank by English Teachers	Rank by Others	Permille Correct by English Teachers	Permille Correct by Others
91. strophe	72	93	97	871	959
92. tabard	33	23	36	333	551
93. timbrel .....(4)*	38	57	30	526	531
94. tutelar	13	5	88	151	878
95. usance	35	32	24	387	469
96. utopian	6	96	99	893	1,000
97. vignette	58	71	71	620	755
98. warlock	15	10	16	204	388
99. wassail	47	89	79	842	816
100. wight ......(8)*)	43	72	70	647	755

In the two tests L_1 and L_2 as finally arranged there are twenty-nine words which are found in the Thorndike list of the 10,000 most important words. (See Thorndike, E. L., *The Teacher's Word Book*.) These words were not selected from the Thorndike list, but were chosen first for their specific contextual settings and later checked in the Thorndike list. They are indicated in these lists by having printed after them the credit-number given in Thorndike's book.

In the Inglis English Tests, Vocabulary, Form A, designed to test the extent of English vocabulary, two out of the 150 words included occur in the two hundred of L_1 and L_2, largesse and sacerdotal. The Inglis was primarily intended for college Freshman.

Pressey's "The Technical Vocabularies of the Public School Subjects," Section 2: *English and American Literature*, said to "contain the technical and comparatively unusual words which are common to textbooks in English and American literature," lists nine of the two hundred words in the tests presented in this study: analogy, aphorism, elegy, epigram, epithet, homily, lexicon, madrigal, vernacular. This list was compiled for use by pupils to assist them n "mastery of the technical terms of a subject" and is recommended for "close study" by the pupils.

APPENDIX D

Order and Difficulty of Words in Final Tests, Forms A and B

Permilles of difficulty and words in order as used in published Form A of Literary Vocabulary Test, composed of the first and fourth of each set of 4 words of the complete list of two hundred words. In order of difficulty as determined by experiment. ($n=406$) [1]

Permille Correct		Permille Correct		Permille Correct	
966	1. nomad	582	34. avouch	394	68. fardel
920	2. catacombs	579	35. apothegm	394	69. panoply
905	3. liege	567	36. hap	389	70. gest
898	4. analogy	564	37. nonce	387	71. savannah
898	5. apocalypse	552	38. apogee	375	72. apologue
871	6. benison	552	39. beldam	367	73. leprechaun
871	7. cynosure	543	40. antiphonal	353	74. corbie
856	8. lucent	543	41. fell	350	75. nadir
856	9. rue	540	42. missal	336	76. immolate
854	10. galleon	540	43. ruth	333	77. corages
842	11. wassail	531	44. timbrel	326	78. paynim
825	12. fain	523	45. bethel	319	79. gloss
822	13. lexicon	518	46. gammer	307	80. ravin
798	14. epigram	513	47. hind	304	81. caravel
791	15. savant	506	48. argosy	285	82. caitiff
762	16. liturgy	506	49. murrain	285	83. pricking
754	17. elegy	496	50. homily	273	84. ruck
735	18. anathema	496	51. minnesinger	270	85. thorp
730	19. bauble	482	52. kismet	248	86. basilisk
725	20. casque	477	53. eke	248	87. quair
723	21. wist	472	54. jongleur	241	88. phylactery
703	22. canny	465	55. jo	219	89. sansculotte
698	23. necromancy	462	56. scrip	204	90. livid
691	24. meed	460	57. springes	204	91. warlock
669	25. dight	450	58. quinquereme	180	92. arrant
657	26. palfrey	445	59. mummer	180	93. gowan
655	27. sibylline	433	60. cavil	163	94. grisly
647	28. wight	431	61. coign	158	95. shawes
640	29. sacerdotal	418	62. fortuitous	151	96. tutelar
633	30. hospice	416	63. quietus	148	97. byre
620	31. asphodel	411	64. nirvana	124	98. lamia
606	32. sedge	409	65. cleped	100	99. rubric
596	33. canticle	409	66. picaroon	58	100. fey
		406	67. scrannel pipes		

[1] Forms A and B are of approximately the same difficulty; total for A—50587; for B—50522.

Appendix

Permilles of difficulty and words in order as used in published Form B of Literary Vocabulary Test composed of the second and third of each set of 4 words of the complete list of two hundred words. In order of difficulty as determined by experiment ($n=406$).

Permille Correct			Permille Correct			Permille Correct		
946	1.	prate	589	34.	seneschal	394	68.	bourn
944	2.	matins	577	35.	connotation	392	69.	berserk
903	3.	vernacular	569	36.	minion	392	70.	spate
900	4.	bacchanal	562	37.	kye	387	71.	usance
893	5.	utopian	557	38.	fen	380	72.	cates
883	6.	boon	552	39.	hegira	365	73.	leal
871	7.	strophe	545	40.	paladin	360	74.	apotheosis
869	8.	saga	540	41.	indenture	350	75.	palter
856	9.	sooth	540	42.	largesse	343	76.	ingle
854	10.	excerpt	533	43.	bucolic	333	77.	tabard
827	11.	palmer	530	44.	epithet	328	78.	barrow
825	12.	arras	523	45.	cabal	314	79.	rede
808	13.	epitome	521	46.	salmagundi	309	80.	obloquy
803	14.	argent	513	47.	posset	304	81.	palimpsest
774	15.	avaunt	509	48.	carl	299	82.	burgeon
769	16.	gargoyle	504	49.	arabesque	273	83.	dithyramb
752	17.	genie	504	50.	flagellate	273	84.	myrmidon
745	18.	orison	496	51.	rathe	263	85.	bole
730	19.	irk	491	52.	chapman	258	86.	arbalest
727	20.	harlequin	476	53.	argot	243	87.	buskin
715	21.	barcarole	472	54.	jeremiad	241	88.	pandect
710	22.	euphuism	465	55.	threnody	214	89.	kermis
696	23.	amulet	462	56.	madrigal	207	90.	mordant
691	24.	anchorite	457	57.	gyve	197	91.	arcana
669	25.	philistine	453	58.	predilection	190	92.	oriflamme
659	26.	anodyne	443	59.	tabor	178	93.	selah
652	27.	eclogue	433	60.	apocryphal	165	94.	orient
650	28.	shibboleth	423	61.	bibliophile	153	95.	avatar
637	29.	aphorism	418	62.	bruit	151	96.	harquebus
637	30.	genre	414	63.	burn	141	97.	kith
620	31.	vignette	411	64.	aegis	129	98.	carline
608	32.	brae	409	65.	cozen	71	99.	contumacious
591	33.	incarnadine	409	66.	hecatomb	58	100.	amerce
			397	67.	caravansary			

APPENDIX E

DATA ON WHICH ALL COMPUTATIONS WERE MADE

The following is an explanatory legend applicable to data upon all groups in Appendix E:

L_1 L_2 L_{av} = Test scores.
Th   = Thorndike Intelligence Examination Part III (1923).
AA   = Army Alpha, Form 7.
Tra = Trabue Measure of Ability in Prose Judging.
Gr   = English mark for one class, one semester.
Deg = College degree in English.
Ex   = Number of years experience in teaching English; 0 = no experience.
Pos = Type of position held: tj = junior high school; t = high school; h = head of department; sup. = supervisor; n. i. = normal instructor; c. i. = college instructor.

Appendix
GROUP A

Case	L_1	L_2	L_{av}	Th	AA	Tra	Gr	Deg	Ex	Pos	Age
1	56	60	58	162	186	21	A	AB	4	h	26
2	38	31	34	112	150	14	C+	AM**	2j	tj	
3	63	67	65	169	176	17	C+	PhD	10	c.i.	
4	45	52	48	124	176	12	C	AB	7j	tj	31
5	53	50	51	160	183	17	B	AB	1	t	
6	80	78	79	174	172	20	B+	AM**	8	t	39
7	79	75	77	184	179	25	A	AM**	0	0	25
8	63	48	55	165	165	16	C+	AB	2	t	
9	84	74	79	204	188	15	A	AM	7	t	
10	30	24	27	121	151	10	D	AB	0	0	23
11	35	35	35	142	162	11	C+	AB	4	t	27
12	70	70	70	191	186	24	A−	AM**	0	0	30
13	42	39	40	137	164	17	C	AB	5	t	30
14	50	42	46	173	190	18	C+	AM**	1	t	25
15	50	52	51	71	143	12	B−	AM**	2	t	27
16	61	49	55	169	167	23	B−	AM	5	t	
17	61	60	60	144	172	22	B	AB	9	t	
18	63	65	64	170	172	18	B	AB	13	t	
19	52	48	50	111	173	11	C+	AB	6	t	
20	35	38	36	124	157	16	C	AB	8	h	34
21	32	41	36	163	153	18	B−	AB	1	t	
22	76	74	75	188	183	18	B	Lit B	0	0	25
23	50	45	48	113	161	19	B−	AM	9	h	33
24	65	74	69	134	168	19	B	AM	3	t	27
25	48	53	51	181	174	16	B+	AB	2	t	24
26	48	39	43	129	150	10	B−	AB	5	t	30
27	59	21	40	58	86	11	D	AM	3½	t	
28	81	78	79	176	178	23	B	PhD	4½	t	
29	58	54	56	135	153	14	B	AM	1	h	31
30	35	46	40	91	166	16	B−	AM**	15	c.i.	
31	67	56	61	164	160	20	B−	AB	tj	tj	28
32	89	85	87	240	168	15	A−	AB*	0	0	
33	41	31	36	105	169	16	C−	AB	6	t	
34	53	49	51	140	175	15	C+	AM	2	t	25
35	56	59	58	65	168	20	B+	AB	3	t	
36	60	65	62	105	177	23	B−	AM	9	t	35
37	52	60	56	131	173	15	C	AB	10	t	
38	50	44	47	121	159	13	C	AB	9	t	35
39	38	30	34	154	183	17	B	AB	½	t	
40	52	41	46	130	164	14	B	AB	3	t	29
41	42	36	39	113	153	10	C	AM	2	h	24
42	83	71	77	211	173	14	A−	AB	0	0	
43	58	50	54	72	113	15	B−	AB	10j	tj	47
44	48	50	49	130	137	11	B	AM	1½	t	
45	43	37	40	105	162	22	B+	AB	5	t	27
46	53	47	50	162	181	18	C	AB	2	t	27
47	31	45	38	180	165	20	C+	AB	5j	tj	
48	63	66	64	215	184	22	B	AB	4	t	26
49	50	49	49	130	167	14	C−	AB	½	t	30
50	41	40	40	128	151	22	B	AB	5	h	
51	37	31	34	84	164	14	C	BS	5	t	33
52	43	36	39	158	187	11	C	AB	2	h	25

* Candidate for, but has not yet received Bachelor's degree.
** Candidate for, but has not yet received Master's degree.

Appendix E

GROUP A (continued)

Case	L_1	L_2	L_{av}	Th	AA	Tra	Gr	Deg	Ex	Pos	Age
53	80	74	77	170	186	24	A	AM**	2	h	
54	27	31	29	77	157	14	D	AB	2½	t	31
55	49	50	49	137	171	12	C	AB	1	t	
56	76	74	75	226	199	19	A −	nor	7	t	35
57	49	46	47	116	138	13	C −	AB	2	t	
58	33	47	40	103	155	19	B −	nor	4j	tj	
59	51	52	51	144	170	22	B −	BS*	3	h	
60	53	48	50	132	168	18	B −	AM**	2	t	24
61	67	74	70	214	194	22	A	BS*	11	h	33
62	48	51	49	162	168	17	C +	AB	0	0	
63	25	30	27	67	121	11	D	AM	0	t	29
64	45	44	44	160	168	15	C	AB	-	t	25
65	59	55	57	159	191	22	B	AM	1½	h	
66	59	55	57	204	187	20	B +	AM	2	t	33
67	16	16	16	124	152	14	C	AB	1	t	
68	67	62	64	204	187	18	B +	BS*	0	0	30
69	38	36	37	198	176	14	C +	AB	0	0	23
70	41	41	41	99	165	13	C +	AM**	8	t	35
71	61	36	48	136	156	13	C	AB	2	t	24
72	70	69	69	169	188	19	B +	AB	5	h	29
73	30	34	32	134	137	15	C	AB	0	0	28
74	48	55	51	112	174	14	B +	AM	24	t	44
75	29	47	38	80	157	15	D	AM**	0	0	
76	51	53	52	132	146	19	C	AM**	1	elem	
77	31	27	29	123	159	8	C	AB	1	h	
78	39	41	40	94	170	12	C −	AM	7	c.i.	45
79	24	24	24	104	138	13	D	AB	4	t	32
80	60	58	59	99	171	17	C +	AB	1	t	24
81	44	47	45	158	148	7	B −	AM	8	h	34
82	56	54	55	170	168	14	C +	AM	1	t	24
83	29	37	33	72	108	9	C	AB	3	t	
84	30	29	29	100	163	21	C	AM**	3j	tj	
85	46	41	43	141	163	19	B	BS*	4	t	25
86	19	27	23	100	119	17	D	BS	1	h	24
87	63	52	57	109	148	19	C +	AM	16	c.i.	48
88	66	70	68	174	179	14	B −	AB	14	h	44
89	36	46	41	145	161	16	B	AB	hs	librarian	35
90	55	62	58	172	177	20	B	AB	3	t	27
91	36	43	39	156	148	15	C	AB	2	t	
92	63	55	59	146	173	16	B −	AB	8	t	44
93	41	39	40	96	131	18	C	AB	4½	t	26
94	82	80	81	146	171	18	A −	AM	13	h	
95	35	42	38	169	164	17	C	AM**	1j	tj	27
96	33	44	38	89	155	14	C	AB	10	t	
97	28	29	28	83	156	13	C −	BS	4	t	
98	42	30	36	173	176	15	C	AB	2	t	24
99	50	58	54	139	157	15	C +	AM	11	t	
100	75	64	69	144	181	15	B +	AM	0	0	31
101	59	56	57	178	179	20	B	AB	½	t	34
102	40	40	40	134	132	15	C	AM	4	t	29
103	36	37	36	89	174	12	C	AM	0	0	
104	42	47	44	118	152	12	C	AB	1	t	

*Candidate for, but has not yet received Bachelor's degree.
**Candidate for, but has not yet received Master's degree.

68 *Appendix*

GROUP A (concluded)

Case	L₁	L₂	Lav	Th	AA	Tra	Gr	Deg	Ex	Pos	Age
105	34	34	34	160	149	15	C	AB	2½	t	
106	33	43	38	104	145	13	C −	AM	12	c.i.	36
107	20	24	22	126	147	10	D	AB	4	h	25
108	35	36	35	97	153	14	B	AM	2	t	36
109	64	59	61	188	170	19	B	AB	15	t	
110	35	44	39	89	155	16	C	AB	8	t	
111	39	40	39	186	133	10	C +	AB	3	t	
112	59	53	56	160	173	15	C +	AM**	1	t	26
113	56	53	54	198	178	6	B	AM	21	nor. sup.	52
114	72	70	71	187	192	16	B	PhB	4	t	
115	35	52	43	60	120	11	C +	AM	10j	tj	43
116	45	46	45	96	163	17	C	AB	4	h	27
117	51	47	49	91	167	14	C +	AB	1j	tj	29
118	39	35	37	80	146	15	C	AB	2	h	25
119	47	45	46	174	183	13	C	AM**	0	0	
120	55	62	58	182	188	15	B	AB	2	t	
121	34	30	32	136	132	14	C	AM	5	t	30
122	55	45	50	130	169	18	B −	AB	0	0	
123	53	46	49	96	167	11	C −	AB	10	t	
124	35	34	34	135	161	18	C +	AB	1	t	
125	36	29	32	139	184	14	C	AM	0	0	27
126	36	50	43	114	172	15	B	AB	1	t	39
127	33	30	31	69	150	9	D	AM	0	0	26
128	43	52	47	150	134	17	C +	AB	6	t	
129	32	38	35	118	127	19	C	AB	2	h	30
130	79	60	69	89	133	13	B −	AB	3	t	26
131	47	42	44	184	153	16	B	AB	0	0	24
132	76	65	70	180	183	22	A −	AB	0	0	
133	25	31	28	111	123	14	C	BS*	3	h	31
134	73	71	72	212	183	23	A	AB	5	h	37
135	52	49	48	197	175	18	B	AM	11	h	
136	71	73	72	170	183	20	C	AB	1	t	22
137	43	41	42	124	161	21	B −	AB	6	t	29
138	49	37	43	138	162	11	C	BS	2	t	29
139	76	67	71	187	182	24	A −	AB	4	t	
140	45	52	48	80	169	14	C	AM**	6	t	
141	42	40	41	140	160	9	C	AM	2j	tj	37
142	32	35	33	170	172	18	C	AB	1	t	27
143	35	36	35	155	164	15	C +	Lit B	3	t	
144	59	57	58	102	172	16	B +	AB	2	t	26
145	33	20	26	79	139	10	D	AB	1	t	
146	46	46	46	153	179	13	B	AB	5	t	30
147	51	46	48	148	150	21	C +	AB	7	t	31
148	80	81	80	164	180	21	A	AB	9	t	
149	28	28	28	68	126	11	D	AB	0	0	
150	23	23	23	82	142	15	C −	AB	3	nor. sup.	24
151	31	33	32	123	176	16	C	AM**	2	t	24
152	33	34	33	118	154	13	C	AM	3	t	29
153	51	52	51	122	168	13	C −	AB	0	0	25
154	60	55	57	144	183	16	B	AM	5	t	
155	44	43	43	117	173	18	C	AB	5	t	

* Candidate for, but has not yet received Bachelor's degree.
**Candidate for, but has not yet received Master's degree.

Appendix E

GROUP B

Case	L_1	L_2	L_{av}	Th	AA	Tra	Gr	Deg	Ex	Pos
1	17	25	21	51	150	14	C	AM	10	t
2	38	37	37	179	149	13	B +	AM	3j	tj
3	76	75	75	190	186	21	A	AB	4	t
4	75	72	73	171	184	22	A −	AB	24	t
5	25	35	30	46	112	6	C +	AM	4	h
6	25	42	33	92	153	15	C +	BS*	6	t
7	24	31	27	68	107	16	C −	AM	8	t
8	32	27	29	84	127	12	C −	AB*	0	0
9	61	57	59	204	175	22	B +	AB	5	t
10	58	55	56	198	181	20	A −	AM	5	t
11	48	47	47	130	162	8	C −	AM	3	t
12	66	62	64	201	180	21	B	AB	½	t
13	41	43	42	199	178	16	B +	AM	5	t
14	59	55	57	139	163	15	B	AB	1	t
15	39	34	36	130	162	16	C −	BS*	6j	tj
16	47	42	44	55½	177	15	C +	AB	2	t
17	78	78	78	126	179	14	B −	AB	0	0
18	35	34	34	151	142	7	C +	AB	0	0
19	56	59	57	170	162	12	B −	AB	2	t
20	52	63	57	130	176	18	A	AM	8	c.i.
21	64	63	63	210	168	19	B −	AM	10	t
22	32	28	30	68	163	11	D	AB	1	t
23	20	26	23	56	79	13	B −	AM	4½	t
24	82	73	77	197	175	22	B +	AM	22	c.i.
25	65	72	68	189	188	22	B	BS	8½	t
26	59	61	60	138	169	19	B +	AB	1	t
27	60	67	63	132	159	15	B −	PhD	11	c.i.
28	55	51	53	170	176	19	B +	AM	15	t
29	47	52	49	168	157	16	B +	AM	1	t
30	34	34	34	131	146	13	F	AM	0	0
31	43	44	43	182	160	16	B	AB	6	t
32	35	39	37	139	174	16	B	AB	6	sup.
33	69	68	68	136	181	20	A	AM**	4	t
34	29	45	37	127	123	21	C	AM	8	t
35	56	42	49	178	184	18	B	AB	1j	tj
36	38	46	42	143	173	14	C	AM	0	0
37	46	49	47	118	167	14	B +	AB	7	t
38	27	27	27	131	150	16	C +	AB	5	t
39	87	86	86	134	180	23	B +	AM	1	t
40	60	64	62	155	161	13	B −	AB	12½	h
41	78	74	76	188	182	21	A	AM	26	h
42	26	36	31	114	151	5	C	BS	4	t
43	71	62	66	174	164	16	B +	AB	8	t
44	53	51	52	175	146	20	B	AB	1	t
45	36	50	43	146	126	14	C	AM	11j	tj
46	40	53	46	72	115	17	B	AB	10½	t
47	32	37	34	136	114	13	C	AB	7	h
48	42	49	45	101	137	15	C	AB	6	t
49	48	43	45	102	152	17	B −	AB	11	t
50	65	65	65	208	197	16	B	BS	0	0
51	14	17	15	71	147	14	C	AM	5	t
52	44	47	45	138	150	11	C	AB	4	t
53	83	77	80	154	168	26	A	BS	13	h
54	93	92	92	250	208	24	A	AB	10	h
55	60	57	58	89	154	14	B	AM	16	t

* Candidate for, but has not yet received Bachelor's degree.
** Candidate for, but has not yet received Master's degree.

70   *Appendix*

GROUP C

Case	L_1	L_2	L_{av}	Th	AA	Tr	Gr	Deg	Ex	Pos
1	34	30	32	116	151	13	B −	AB	0	0
2	74	82	78	196	182	21	A	AB	6	t
3	33	40	36	90	159	18	C	AM	0	0
4	57	53	55	168	179	17	B	AB*	0	0
5	42	40	41	105	133	12	C	AB	0	0
6	41	51	46	140	162	13	B −	AM	0	0
7	31	44	37	79	131	15	C	AM	2	t
8	66	55	60	118	162	13	B +	AB	0	0
9	23	37	30	131	160	17	B	AM**	ij	tj
10	26	39	32	103	130	16	C	AM**	i	t
11	85	83	84	186	160	20	A	AB	11	t
12	21	29	25	59	108	14	C −	AM	0	0
13	33	33	33	150	162	18	C +	AM	2j	tj
14	67	64	65	137	179	18	A −	AB	3	t
15	28	33	30	96	148	18	C +	BS*	0	0
16	42	43	42	81	140	21	C +	AM	12	c.i.
17	42	47	44	158	163	21	B −	AB	0	0
18	53	53	55	181	167	17	B −	AB*	0	0
19	59	44	51	98	148	16	C	AB*	0	0
20	32	41	36	94	171	19	C	BS*	7j	t
21	38	40	39	132	160	13	B −	n.s.	3	t
22	59	68	63	150	151	15	B −	AM	5	t
23	81	79	80	180	176	19	A −	AM**	0	0
24	50	52	51	164	174	26	B +	AB	0	0
25	65	64	64	200	171	22	B −	AM	1c	c.i.
26	40	45	42	146	160	17	B −	AM	3	t
27	38	39	38	77	82	13	B −	AM	2¼	t
28	83	79	81	212	178	22	B	AM	4	sup.
29	48	50	49	95	187	17	B	AB*	0	0
30	23	19	21	83	142	17	C −	AM	4	t
31	43	42	42	170	157	25	B −	AM**	0	0
32	33	42	37	126	180	20	B	AB	0	0
33	19	25	22	117	160	14	C	AB	0	0
34	69	65	67	200	171	22	B +	AM	8	h
35	58	70	64	148	155	17	B +	AB	3	h
36	33	29	31	136	140	12	C	AM	0	0
37	24	27	25	125	139	21	C −	AM	0	0
38	37	36	36	104	165	24	C +	AM	1	t
39	41	40	40	82	123	18	B +	AM	4	c.i.
40	45	32	38	115	127	16	B −	AB	0	0
41	32	35	33	127	145	19	B	AB	2	h
42	40	36	38	75	115	13	C −	AM	15	n.i.
43	69	55	62	196	181	18	A	AB	0	0
44	87	84	85	153	182	25	A	AB	11	t
45	31	34	32	89	126	23	B −	AM	6	n.i.
46	56	48	52	133	160	14	B	AB	10	t
47	81	70	75	214	170	19	C +	AB	0	0
48	57	57	57	72	116	15	B −	AM**	8	t
49	50	45	47	108	156	20	B −	AB	0	0
50	44	43	43	118	171	14	C +	AB*	0	0
51	62	62	62	181	144	21	A	BS*	2j	tj
52	24	36	30	192	156	20	C −	AB	0	0
53	26	39	32	101	142	15	C −	AB*	1	t

* Candidate for, but has not yet received Bachelor's degree.
** Candidate for, but has not yet received Master's degree.

Appendix E

GROUP C (*concluded*)

Case	L_1	L_2	L_{av}	Th	AA	Tr	Gr	Deg	Ex	Pos
54	40	48	44	124	136	11	B −	AB	0	0
55	31	36	33	66	125	15	C	AB	1	t
56	13	16	14	51	79	11	C	AM	0	0
57	15	32	23	99	159	22	C +	AB	0	0
58	52	53	52	120	141	21	C +	AM	9	h
59	51	45	48	148	179	13	C +	AM	1½ j	tj
60	36	38	37	125	128	10	C	AM**	0	0
61	69	53	61	199	191	18	B	AB*	0	0
62	38	30	34	172	143	15	C	AM	1½	t
63	69	76	72	117	159	16	B −	AM	7	c.i.

* Candidate for, but has not yet received Bachelor's degree.
** Candidate for, but has not yet received Master's degree.

Appendix

GROUP D

Case	L₁	L₂	Lₐᵥ	Th	AA	Gr	Dept. Ex.	Deg	Exp	Pos
1	69	31	50			B –		AB	0	0
2	58	61	59		162	B –		AM	0	0
3	41	35	38	163	162	B		AM	10	t
4	41	39	40			C		BS*	2	tj
5	40	32	36			B	180	AM	3	t
6	37	36	36			B –		AM**	0	0
7	42	39	40			B –		AB	11	tj
8	70	62	66			A –	213	AM**	24	tj
9	64	57	60	80	111	B		AM	7	t
10	31	39	35			C +	177	AB	5	t
11	45	46	45		173	B	196	AM	5	t
12	48	48	48	128	176	B –		AB	8	t
13	56	65	60			B +	192	AM	4	n.i.
14	42	41	41	196	168	B –		AB	0	0
15	66	70	68			B –		PhD	11	c.i.
16	48	49	48			C +		AM	7	c.i.
17	49	54	51			A –	186	AB	2	t
18	20	15	17			B –		AB	0	0
19	63	60	61			B –		AM	0	0
20	54	53	53		136	B		AB	0	0
21	38	38	38			B –		AM	4½	h
22	17	12	14			C		BS*	0	0
23	50	61	55			C		AB	4	t
24	39	30	34			B	166	AB	3	t
25	47	47	47		132	F		MS**	0	0
26	74	69	71			B +	192	AM**	7	t
27	47	46	46			B –		AB	5	t
28	39	47	43	118	138	B +	155	AM*	5	t
29	26	25	25			B	154	AB	0	0
30	36	36	36		122	B		AM	19	n.i.
31	26	25	25			B		BS	2	t
32	85	80	75			A –		AM	0	0
33	42	46	44			B	177	AB	2	t
34	79	76	77	170	170	C +	201	PhB	14	t
35	75	65	70	198	169	B –		AM	8	h
36	35	36	35			A –		AB*	0	0
37	52	52	52			B +		AB	6	t
38	41	41	41	116	150	B –		BS*	1	tj
39	24	33	28			C –	110	AM	6	h
40	56	52	54			B		AB	0	0
41	83	68	75	178	188	B +		AB	3	t
42	74	51	62	136	169	B		AM	3	c.i.
43	74	58	66			B +		AB	3	t
44	27	34	30			B –	149	AM	10	c.i.
45	69	54	61		175	B +		AM	9	n.i.
46	36	37	36	130	149	B	175	AB	5	t
47	46	46	46		144	B +		BS*	4	h
48	47	41	44			B +		AB*	0	0
49	37	29	33			B +		AB*	0	0
50	33	30	31			B		AB	0	0
51	33	23	28	148	155	C		AB	3	t
52	26	30	28			B		AB	0	0
53	54	50	52			A –	175	AM	6	h
54	58	46	52	125	104	B		AB	0	0
55	26	37	31			B –		AM	2	tj
56	45	45	45			B –		AM**	0	0

* Candidate for, but has not yet received Bachelor's degree.
** Candidate for, but has not yet received Master's degree.

Appendix E

GROUP E

Case	L_1	L_2	L_{av}	Th	AA	Gr	Tr	Dept. Ex.	Deg.	Ex	Pos	Age
1	37	22	29	78	139	C	13	112	AM	2	t	27
2	41	51	46	140	162	B −	13	148	AM	0	0	24
3	39	41	40	134	168	B −	17	101	AM	0	0	
4	42	39	40	137	164	C	17	160	AB	5	t	30
5	23	37	30	131	160	B	17	122	AM**	1	tj	24
6	38	39	38	150	163	C −	18	135	AM	0	0	20
7	33	33	33	150	162	C +	18	170	AM	2	tj	22
8	67	64	65	137	179	A −	18	208	AB	3	t	32
9	32	41	36	94	171	C	19	145	BS*	7	tj	40
10	20	26	23	56	79	B −	13	101	AM	4½	t	43
11	59	68	63	150	151	B −	15	176	AM	5	t	29
12	81	79	80	180	176	A −	19	196	AM	0	0	25
13	47	39	43	87	142	B	14	146	AM**	1	t	25
14	43	42	42	170	157	B −	25	161	AM**	0	0	24
15	69	65	67	200	171	B +	22	182	AM	8	h	29
16	58	70	64	148	155	B +	17	153	AB	3	h	24
17	24	24	24	104	138	D	13	184	AB	4	t	32
18	33	29	31	136	140	C	12	130	AM	0	0	27
19	24	27	25	125	139	C −	21	96	AM	0	0	23
20	41	40	40	82	123	B +	18	197	AM	4	c.i	23
21	37	36	36	104	165	C +	24	151	AM	1	t	
22	32	35	33	127	145	B	19	151	AB	2	h	24
23	40	36	38	75	115	C −	13	149	AM	15	n.i.	48
24	69	55	62	196	181	A	18	194	AB	0	0	22
25	35	36	35	97	153	B	14	133	AM	2	t	36
26	87	84	85	153	182	A	25	226	AB	11	t	35
27	31	34	32	89	126	B −	23	156	AM	6	n.i.	31
28	45	46	45	96	163	C	17	154	AB	4	t	27
29	56	48	52	133	160	B	14	159	AB	10	n.i.	37
30	69	76	72	117	159	B −	16	191	AM	7	c.i.	32
31	62	62	62	181	144	A −	21	194	BS*	2	tj	46
32	26	39	32	101	142	C −	15	156	AB*	1	t	25
33	9	29	19	82	127	F	15	132	AM	0	0	22
34	13	16	14	51	79	C	11	104	AM	0	0	26
35	52	53	52	120	141	C +	21	191	AM	9	h	35
36	69	53	61	199	191	B	18	172	AB*	0	0	

* Candidate for, but has not yet received Bachelor's degree.
** Candidate for, but has not yet received Master's degree.

Appendix

GROUP F

Case	L_1	L_2	L_{av}	Th	AA	Tr	Gr	Dept. Ex.	Deg	Exp	Pos
1	56	60	58	162	186	21	A	$150\frac{1}{2}$	AB	4	h
2	76	75	75	190	186	21	A	$152\frac{1}{4}$	AB	4	t
3	80	78	79	174	172	20	B +	$147\frac{3}{4}$	AM**	8	t
4	58	55	56	198	181	20	A −	$119\frac{1}{4}$	AM	6	t
5	50	45	47	113	161	19	B −	$107\frac{1}{4}$	AM	9	h
6	67	56	61	164	160	20	B −	129	AB	1	tj
7	35	34	34	151	142	7	C +	$95\frac{1}{4}$	AB	1	tj
8	52	63	57	130	176	18	A	$140\frac{1}{2}$	AM	8	n.i.
9	64	63	63	210	168	19	B −	$133\frac{1}{2}$	AM	10	tj
10	80	74	77	170	186	24	A	$162\frac{1}{2}$	AM**	21	h
11	67	74	70	214	194	22	A	$156\frac{1}{4}$	BS*	11	h
12	45	44	44	160	168	15	C	113	AB	2	t
13	59	55	57	159	191	22	B	$134\frac{1}{4}$	AM	$7\frac{1}{2}$	h
14	67	62	64	204	187	18	B +	$143\frac{1}{2}$	BS*	0	0
15	82	80	81	146	171	18	A −	$164\frac{1}{2}$	AM	13	h
16	47	45	46	174	183	13	C	132	AM**	0	0
17	76	67	71	187	182	24	A −	$156\frac{1}{4}$	AB	4	t
18	32	35	33	170	172	18	C	124	AB	1	t
19	93	92	92	250	208	24	A	$179\frac{3}{4}$	AB	10	h

* Candidate for, but has not yet received Bachelor's degree.
** Candidate for, but has not yet received Master's degree.

GROUP G

Case	L_1	L_2	L_{av}	Deg	Exp	Pos
1	67	64	65	AB	3	c.i.
2	51	53	52	AB	$4\frac{1}{2}$	h
3	76	74	75	AB	1	tj
4	84	88	86	AM	20	h
5	67	56	61	AB	8	t
6	61	51	56	AB	3	n.i.
7	36	25	30	AM	5	tj
8	70	65	67	AM*	8	n.i.
9	66	62	64	AB	6	t
10	63	67	65	AM	$4\frac{1}{2}$	c.i.
11	86	79	82	AM*	$14\frac{1}{2}$	n.i.
12	85	78	81	AM	16	h
13	87	84	85	AB	11	h
14	80	90	85	AB	$8\frac{1}{2}$	h
15	75	65	70	AM	8	h
16	79	91	85	AM	12	t
17	51	61	56	AB	2	h
18	78	70	74	AB	2	t
19	72	54	63	AM*	$6\frac{1}{2}$	tj

* Candidate for, but has not yet received Master's degree.

Appendix E

GROUP H

Case	L_1	L_2	L_{av}	Deg	Exp	Pos
1	90	71	80	AM	5	t
2	78	77	77	BS	13	t
3	80	80	80	AM	10	t
4	73	74	73	AM	10	t
5	96	91	93	AM	16	t
6	88	70	79	AM	20	t
7	45	48	46	AB	5	t
8	83	78	80	AB	21	t
9	82	70	76	AM	9	t
10	77	77	77	AB	15	t
11	85	87	86	AB	29	t
12	88	84	86	AM	27	t
13	65	57	61	AB	0	0
14	79	75	77	AM*	7	t
15	89	79	84	AB	1	t
16	88	87	87	BS	18	t
17	89	84	86	AM	14	t
18	71	58	64	AM	27	t
19	54	45	49	AB	1	t
20	72	70	71	AM	20	t
21	80	66	73	AB	7	t
22	63	60	61	AB	2	t
23	75	78	76	AM	14	t
24	90	97	93	AB	6½	t
25	68	66	67	AB	4	t
26	78	69	73	AM	14	t
27	84	88	86	AM	20	h

* This is a candidate for the degree of Ph. D.

Appendix

GROUP I

Case	L_1	L_2	L_{av}
1	72	75	73
2	59	59	59
3	61	56	58
4	53	50	51
5	40	39	39
6	82	85	83
7	45	51	48
8	60	65	62
9	78	72	75
10	32	35	33
11	84	82	83
12	66	79	72
13	82	71	76
14	88	92	90
15	52	48	50
16	65	63	64
17	76	76	76
18	66	57	61
19	69	63	66
20	56	50	53
21	70	52	61
22	59	78	68
23	75	70	72
24	43	40	41
25	52	50	51
26	39	39	39
27	42	48	45
28	66	81	73
29	64	72	68
30	92	90	91
31	86	85	85
32	66	72	69
33	71	68	69
34	50	46	48
35	90	85	87
36	44	48	46
37	52	47	49
38	32	29	30
39	54	56	55
40	83	84	83
41	31	23	27
42	62	67	64
43	54	59	55
44	89	77	83
45	65	63	64
46	70	64	67
47	71	65	68
48	34	36	35
49	71	71	71

BIBLIOGRAPHY

ABBOTT, ALLAN. "Standards for the English Teacher." *The English Journal*, Feb., 1922.
BAKER, FRANKLIN T. "The Teacher of English." *The English Journal*, June, 1913.
BURD, H. A. "English Literature Courses in the Small College." *The English Journal*, Feb., 1914.
CARPENTER, BAKER and SCOTT. *The Teaching of English*. Longmans, 1903.
CHUBB, PERCIVAL. *The Teaching of English*. Macmillan, 1903.
DEWEY, JOHN. *How We Think*. D. C. Heath and Company, 1910.
FAIRCHILD, A. H. R. "The Sequence of Courses for College and University Students who Choose English as a Major Subject." *The English Journal*, March, 1923.
GAW, ALLISON. "The Collegiate Training of the Teacher of High School English." *The English Journal*, May, 1916.
GERLACH, F. M. *Vocabulary Studies*. Studies in Education and Psychology, Colorado College, No. 1, 1917.
INGLIS, ALEXANDER. *Principles of Secondary Education*. Houghton Mifflin Company, 1918.
KELLEY, T. L. *Statistical Method*. The Macmillan Company, 1923.
LEONARD, S. A. *Essential Principles of Teaching Reading and Literature*. Lippincott, 1922.
NOBLE, S. G. "The Duplication of Elementary and Secondary Subject-Matter in College English." *The English Journal*, January, 1923.
PAUL, H. G. *The Preparation of High School Teachers of English*. The Bulletin of the Illinois Association of Teachers of English, Feb. 15, 1915.
PRESSEY, L. C. *The Technical Vocabularies of the Public School Subjects*, Section 2, Public School Publishing Co.
Report, *Committee on the Preparation of High School Teachers of English*, 1915.
Report of the National Committee on Reading. *The Twenty-Fourth Yearbook of the National Society for the Study of Education*, Part I. Public School Publishing Co., 1925.
Report, *Reorganization of English in Secondary Schools*. Department of the Interior, Bureau of Education, Bulletin, 1917, No. 2.
Report, *The Teaching of English in Large Cities of the United States*. New York City Association of Teachers of English, Oct., 1922.
TERMAN, L. M. *The Intelligence of School Children*. Houghton Mifflin Co., 1919.
TERMAN, L. M. *The Measurement of Intelligence*. Houghton Mifflin Co., 1916.
TERMAN, KOHS, S. C., and OTHERS. "The Vocabulary Test as a Measure of Intelligence." *Journal of Educational Psychology*, Oct., 1918.
THOMAS, C. S. *The Teaching of English in the Secondary School*. Houghton Mifflin Co., 1917.

THOMSON, GODFREY H. *Instinct, Intelligence, and Character.* Longmans, 1925.

THORNDIKE, E. L. Instructions for Giving, Scoring and Interpreting Scores, Thorndike Intelligence Examination for High School Graduates. Series 1925-1930. Bureau of Publications, Teachers College, Columbia University, 1924.

THORNDIKE, E. L. *The Teacher's Word Book.* Bureau of Publications, Teachers College, Columbia University, 1921.

THORNDIKE, E. L. *Vocabularies of School Pupils.* Contributions to Education, Vol. I, p. 74, of the New York Society for Experimental Study of Education, 1924.

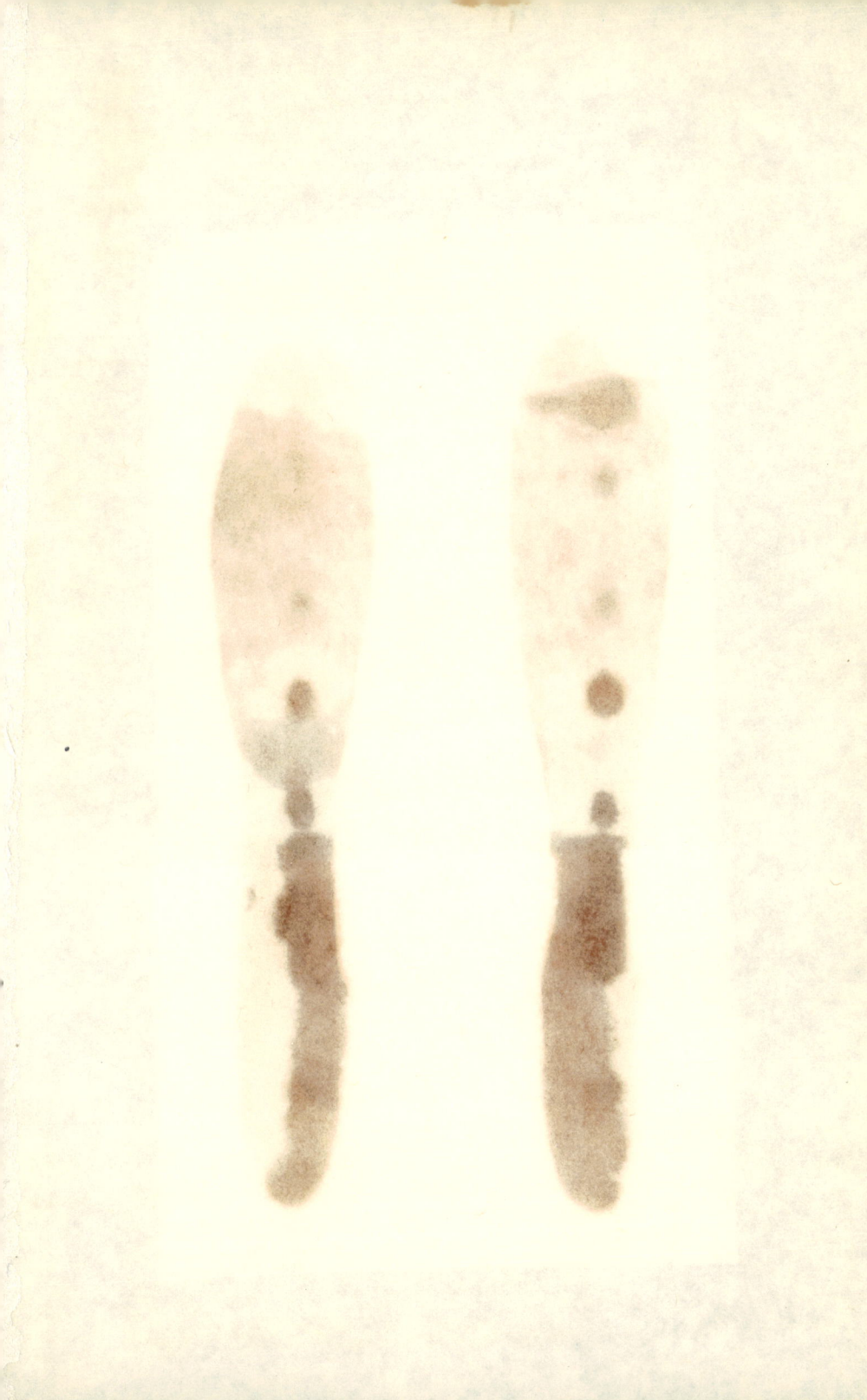

DATE DUE			
MAR 1 9 1981			
FEB 23 '81			

61-950 PRINTED IN U.S.A.

PR
35
.K4
1972

80-4600

Kennon, Laura Hall Vere, 1888–

Tests of literary vocabulary for teachers of English

WITHDRAWN

PJC LEARNING RESOURCES CENTER